By the same author

Naked and Unashamed: Nudism from Six Points of

The Naked Truth about Nudism

available from
wolfbaitbooks.com

First published in 1937
This edition published in 2024
by Wolfbait Books
www.wolfbait.co.uk

A CIP record for this book is available from the British Library
ISBN: 978-1-917298-02-5 (hardback)
ISBN: 978-1-917298-03-2 (ebook)

IT'S ONLY NATURAL

THE PHILOSOPHY OF NUDISM

By William Welby

Foreword by Mark Storey

Photographs by Stephen Glass

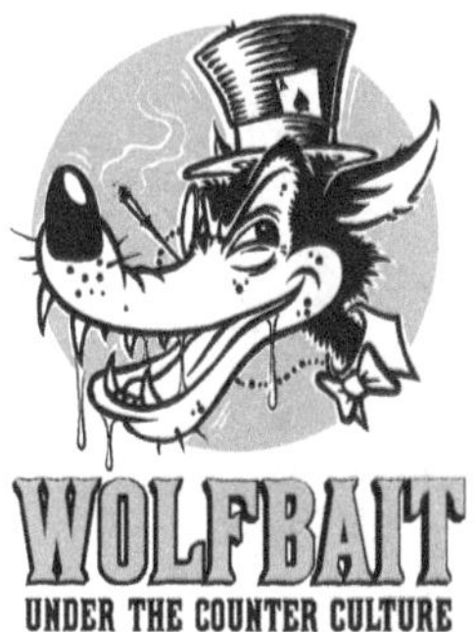

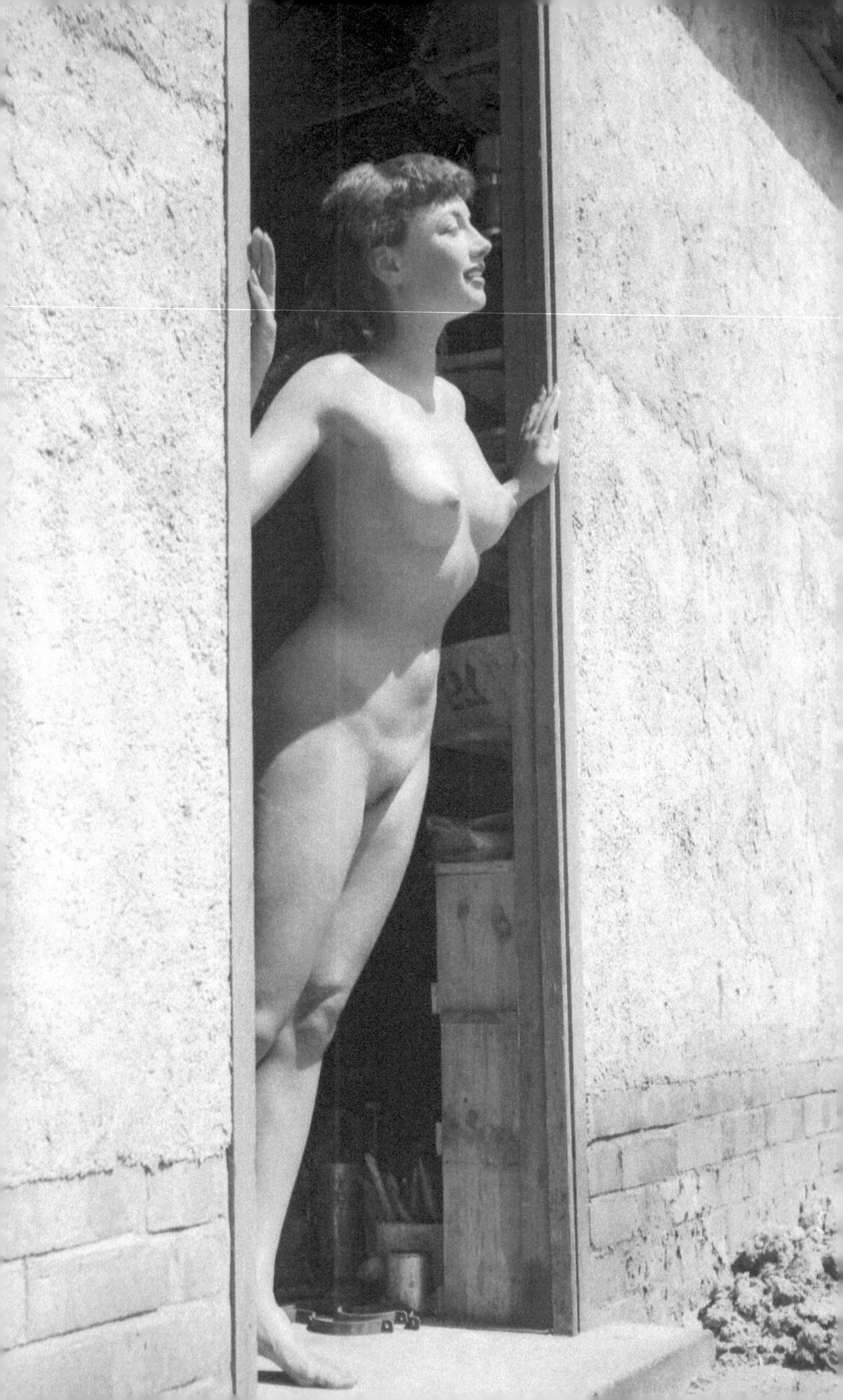

Contents

	PAGE
Foreword by Mark Storey	9

Chapter I
"It's Only Natural" 13

Chapter II
The Tyranny of Fashion 23

Chapter III
"Back to Nature" 33

Chapter IV
Nature's Needs 43

Chapter V
Body and Soul 53

Chapter VI
Natural Selection 63

Chapter VII
Nudity in Fiction 74

Chapter VIII
The Philosophy of Nudism 86

Left: *Ready to Explore*. Pamela Green.

"When I cast off my clothes, I cast off my cares."
Horace Walpole (English diplomat and politician)

Illustrations
by Stephen Glass

PAGE

Ready to Explore 4

Cheeky! 8

"Want to push?" 17

Ready, Steady, Go! 30

Artemis 49

The Elusive Dryad 60

Pose and Poise 70

Calm Waters 82

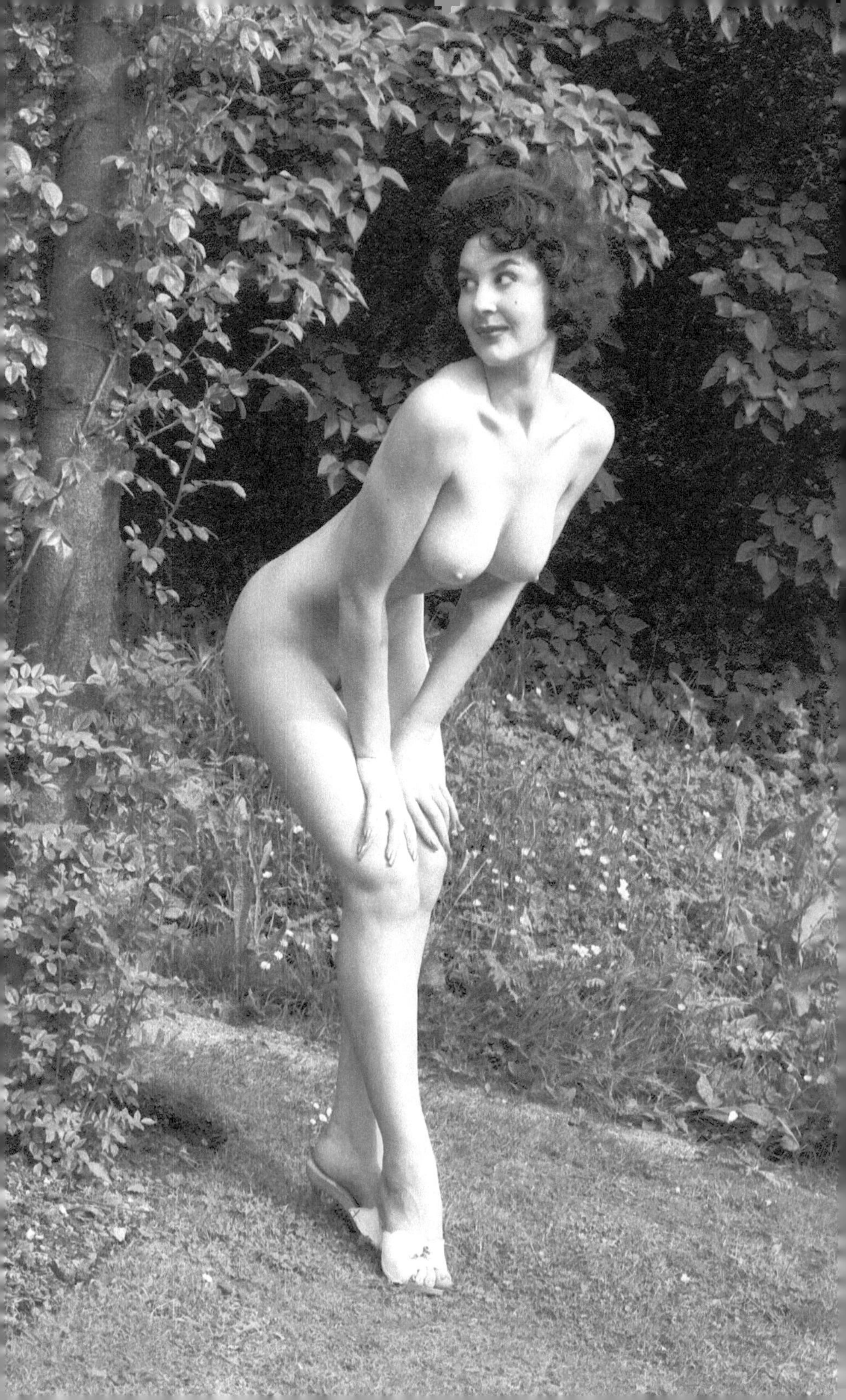

Foreword

WILLIAM WELBY WAS one of England's earliest public voices for naturism. He referred to himself as a "nudist", as was common in the United Kingdom in the 1930s. He openly championed and participated in the movement, culminating in the authorship of three books on the subject under his own name. This set him apart from many British pioneers of naturism, who opted for pseudonyms in print and within their nudist communities.

Welby wrote his three books on nudism in rapid succession, each released by London's Thorsons Publishers. The first was *Naked and Unashamed: Nudism from Six Points of View* (1934), written after researching nudism thoroughly but without experiencing it firsthand. He aimed to provide an objective appraisal of outdoor social nudity, without heavy-handed argument. The book proved popular, and upon its release he received numerous invitations to visit various British nudist clubs. He and his wife Hilda did so with their children, and immediately came to love it. In his second book, *The Naked Truth about Nudism* (1935), Welby thus could take a second stance: of a nudist personally familiar with social nudity, again forgoing proselytization. In his third and final book on nudism, *It's Only Natural: The Philosophy of Nudism* (1937), he speaks as a seasoned nudist with "several" years of clothes-free experience. The three books don't need to be read in order, as each makes an individual case for nudist life from

Left: *Cheeky!* Grace Jackson.

a different voice, calmly considering an activity that society (then as today) tended to regard as a bit odd.

Noteworthy is Welby's tone. If any words sum up his manner of presenting the strengths and potential pitfalls of nudism, they are "commonsense" and "sensible". He concludes *Naked and Unashamed* with a chapter entitled "The Commonsense Point of View", and in *The Naked Truth about Nudism* he routinely states how "sensible" nudism is. In *It's Only Natural,* he develops this theme in every chapter. And he was not alone in this view among the writers on nudism of the 1930s. George Ryley Scott published *The Commonsense of Nudism* (London: T. Werner Laurie) in 1934, and I. O. Evans published *Sensible Sun-Bathing* (Thorsons Publishers) in 1935. There was something about the 1930s British mindset that was attracted to commonsense, and Welby was in the thick of it.

In his opening chapter of *It's Only Natural*, Welby says, "I hope the actual experiences of myself and my friends will be admitted to be at least as convincing as any mere theory advanced by those lacking either experience or understanding." He then offers a series of appeals to commonsense to show that when looked at dispassionately, the physical and psychological benefits of nudism make it worth considering. If, after careful consideration, readers opt not to take part, then so be it. Nudism is not for everyone, and "authentic" nudists are sensible enough not to push it on others. Welby is clearly playing to a very specific audience. He's not writing for academics or students seeking a detailed history of British nudism. He's addressing the man and woman on the street who want nothing to do with quirky fads, fanaticism, or cultish behaviour. Fortunately, according to Welby, nudism is nothing like that… it's sensible.

British philosophers of the time were sounding a similar call. G. E. Moore was making a name for himself in higher academic circles, responding to anti-intuitive, sceptical positions that challenged our knowledge of everyday objects. Moore argued that it's clear we have hands, and we thereby know that we have hands. Scepticism regarding the external world can thus be dismissed. On a more popular level, C. E. M. Joad became a well-known British intellectual with his written articles and radio shows, and later with his participation in the BBC's *The Brains Trust*. Joad viewed his audience as ordinary, thoughtful people, and made philosophy down-to-earth, applicable, and relevant to everyday experience. British audiences loved him for it. Welby did the same thing in his nudist books, and they therefore sold well, each going through multiple editions and printings.

Welby did not limit his writing to the subject of nudism. Thorsons also published his *Mind Your Mind: Simple Psychology for the Layman* (1941), *More Than Bread: A Guide to the Achievement of Success and Happiness* (1943), and *Bending the Twig: A Guide to the Building of To-morrow's Citizens* (1948). In the first book's chapter titled "Business Psychology", he writes from his experience of more than two decades working as a London advertising copywriter and editor, claiming that commonsense and empathy more effectively sell a position than being one-sided and dogmatic: "Sometimes mere doggedness and repetition will wear down opposition and secure the desired result, but more often subtlety and agreeability win the day. If a customer feels that the salesman is just trying to make

a sale, he immediately builds up a barrier of self-protection —
what is known in the jargon of so-called sales psychologists as
'consumer resistance'. To be successful it is essential to 'read the
mind' of the other party; to see how the proposal put forward
will appear to them: to 'see the customer's point of view' and
to anticipate any objections likely to be raised."

It's Only Natural is an easygoing appraisal of nudism's
benefits, as they were understood in 1930s England. What
readers will not find is the voice of a crazed prophet of nudity.
If nothing else, Welby will appear rather sensible.

Mark Storey
Consulting editor, *Nude & Natural* magazine.
Author, *Cinema au Natural: A History of Nudist Film.*

CHAPTER 1

"It's Only Natural"

MANY PEOPLE STILL seem to think that the practice of Nudism is confined to cranks and faddists. Nothing could be further from the truth. Nudists are no more extraordinary than cyclists or motorists. Most of them are, in fact, very ordinary people and essentially natural; that is why they are attracted by the Movement. A "solo-flight" by a young woman in an aeroplane to Australia, South Africa, or even across the Atlantic, is now regarded with comparatively little excitement. Passengers fly regularly to all parts of the Continent with less ado than our ancestors travelled fifty miles by railway, and a mile a minute by motor car is considered a "comfortable cruising speed" by modern motorists. Indeed, compared with over 300 miles per hour on Daytona Beach it is neither alarming nor thrilling; it is taken quite as a matter of course. In my young days, Jules Verne let his fancy play upon travel under the sea in a submarine vessel, and while schoolboys revelled in the wild flights of his imagination, they were thought merely mildly amusing by the elders. To-day, every maritime nation of the world has a fleet of submarines growing greater, both in numbers and in size, day by day. Modern science has brought us "wireless," silk made from wood, "talkies," artificially-preserved foods and — poison gas. And all these things we have grown to look upon as quite natural.

If, on the other hand, groups of people gather together to sun-bathe, exercise or play games unclothed, the general public regard them as extraordinary creatures who are either depraved, mentally unstable or "unnatural." Considered coolly and deliberately, which is more natural? We are all born without clothes, and some of the finest physical specimens of the human race wear little or no clothes to-day. Children delight in shedding their clothes at every opportunity; it is natural to them until they have been taught to the contrary. What can be more natural than animals? They do not wear clothes. When physical exertion is called for, it is only natural to discard as much clothing as possible. The athlete strips down to light shorts and vest or mere slips. The workman throws off coat, waistcoat, collar, and very often shirt as well. It is only natural. The well-to-do and cultured classes of both sexes seek similar freedom when they wish to relax. The man slips into a dressing gown, and the woman dons a loose wrapper or negligee. Instinct tells them that they cannot be really comfortable wrapped up in a number of tightly fitting shells or coverings, because this is *not* natural. Custom and convention decree that we shall cover our bodies in public — not for warmth, not for protection, but for decency. I suppose in some circles it would be held as bordering on indecency to wear a black tie with a full dress suit, or to wear a hat with an evening gown. But these things are purely conventional, mere phases of fashion — man-made laws which may be changed according to whim, while the laws of Nature are immutable.

It is begging the question to claim that after many generations of unnatural living we must continue to live unnaturally. Perhaps — most probably, in fact — we have depreciated many of our natural faculties of protection against disease, fatigue, cold and heat. Over-heated rooms and railway carriages, excess of clothing and unsuitable diets, have much to answer for. Yet, in spite of all these, it is wonderful what can be done by giving Nature a reasonable chance to recuperate. It is said that "you cannot change Human Nature." Never was there a greater fallacy, and this is proved by the fact that human beings born and bred in temperate zones become acclimatised to both the torrid tropics and the frigid borders of the Arctic circles. Human beings thrive under changed climatic conditions which would cause animals to die and plants to wither into nothingness. The fact that the civilised races of the world exist to-day is proof of Man's adaptability. Allowing for the many and varied modifications through which mankind has passed during the centuries, however, the fundamental bases of human physiology remain. The chemical composition of the body remains unchanged and the physiological requirements are the same. Nature demands that a suitable amount of oxygen shall be absorbed by way of the lungs and through the pores of the skin. The lungs cannot obtain sufficient oxygen in a stuffy atmosphere, and the skin cannot absorb oxygen if muffled in layers of clothing. The chemical effects of light are completely cut off while the body is covered, and with most people the body is covered continually.

When my wife and her sister were at a Convent School they took their bath in the usual way, but a Sister who entered the bath-room was terribly shocked to see them naked and quickly produced two large sheet-like garments which covered them from neck to foot, and they had to finish washing themselves, as best they might, under these covers. The average individual who has not really considered these things, fails to realise how utterly artificial is this continuous swaddling of the body. The work which the skin has to do, and which it cannot do without light and air, is seldom understood. The skin is an active organ in the same sense as the heart and the lungs and the stomach. It has certain duties to perform which should be encouraged instead of stultified, and it needs light and air as much as a plant. The average man does not think much about his health until he has lost it. A cold, influenza, indigestion or similar indisposition then drives him to remember advertisements of quack medicines or household remedies recommended by friends; but modern medical science is concentrating more and more on the *prevention* of disease, and this is best accomplished by living naturally. One of the requisites of natural living is periodical exposure of the body to light and air — preferably natural sunshine in an unpolluted atmosphere. Nudists know this, and it is the principal reason why the Movement has grown so rapidly in England, Germany, America and France. It has led the way to a more natural life generally. More fresh air and exercise in the open, simpler food, and exposure to the almost miraculous proper-ties of the ultra-violet, infra-red and other rays. A well-tanned skin is usually free from cutaneous blemishes and accompanied by bright eyes and alert movements.

There is a certain technique about even so simple a practice as sun-bathing. Over-exposure before the skin is properly acclimatised is definitely harmful, and the sufferings of over-zealous beginners are often used as arguments against Nudism. Veterans with a good protective coat of tan can work or play

---

Right: *"Want to push?"* Audrey Wayne.

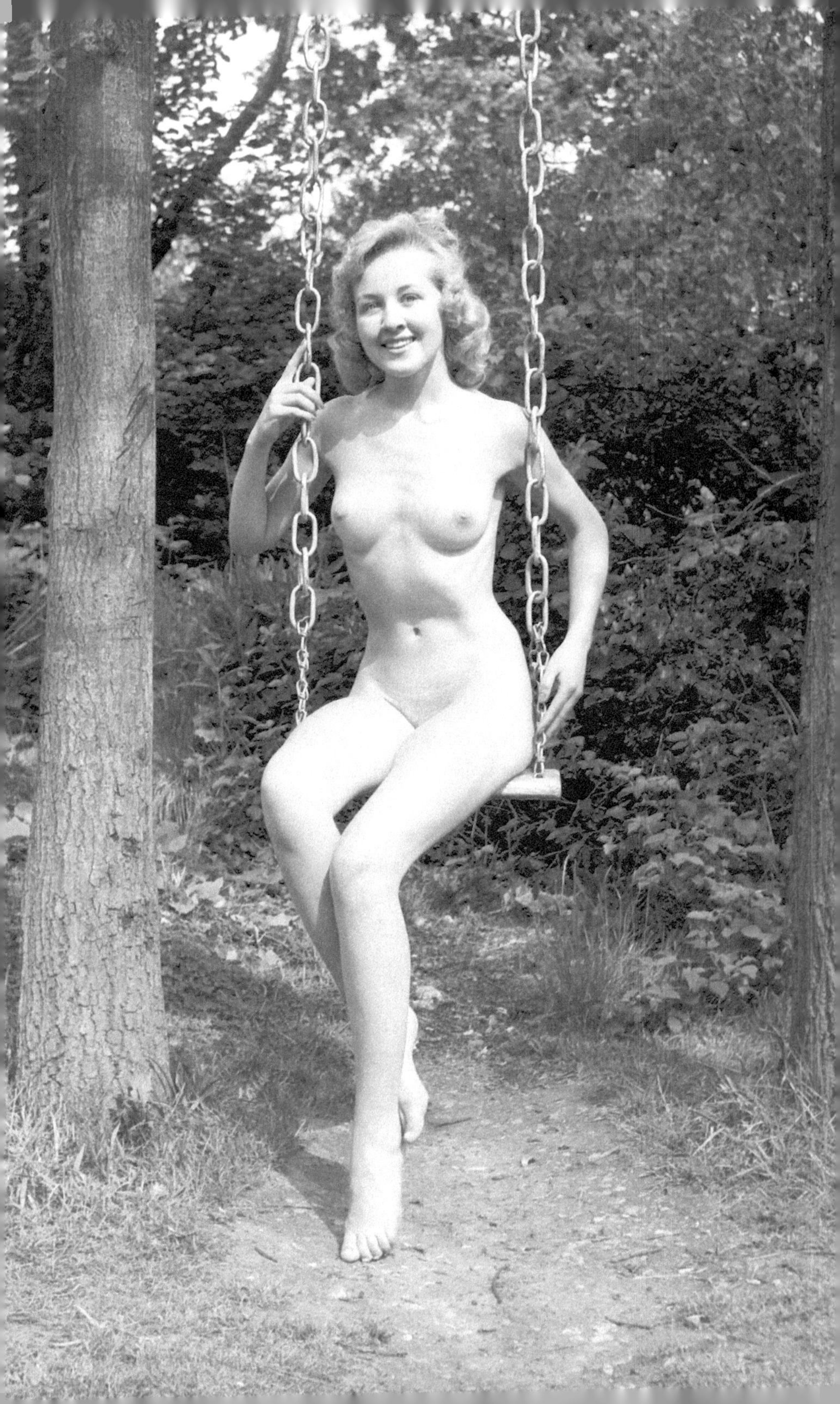

all day in strong sunlight, but the novices must have patience and be satisfied with short and gradual exposures. The skin having lost some of its protective properties through prolonged inaction must be cultivated to ensure its natural efficiency. The head and back of the neck particularly should be kept covered in very hot sunshine, and the body kept in movement as much as possible. Under a bright blue sky the body will become tanned in time without direct exposure to the sun, and the novice should at first concentrate on "air-bathing" rather than actual sun-bathing. Almost invariably a short course of such exposures produces a general improvement in health and a sense of well-being.

I speak with some authority as I and my family are Nudists of several years' standing and I have associated with some hundreds of men, women and children who bear witness to the beneficial effects of their practice. Perhaps, at this date, it is hardly necessary for me to stress the benefit to health to be gained by complete exposure of the body to sun and air. During the last year or two, eminent medical men have added their testimony as to the value of the ultra-violet and infra-red rays, of proper ventilation of the skin and the need for physical culture such as may be obtained in a Nudist camp, under the supervision of a qualified instructor. Our Ministry of Health has awakened to the need for an "A.1 nation," and steps are being taken in various directions to attain such an ideal. There remains, however, the common prejudice to be overcome by those without experience and with only a limited understanding of what Nudism really means. It should not be necessary, so late in the day, to explain that Nudists are respectable people who get no sexual thrill out of seeing each other unclothed.

There never was the slightest foundation for such a misunderstanding, as anyone of ordinary intelligence will see on sensible consideration of the facts. Nudists are drawn from all classes, including Church of England and Nonconformist clergymen, and among them are many highly-respected members of public and business institutions. They find it natural and pleasant to relieve themselves of their clothes on occasion, and have neither fear nor reluctance in telling their friends so. Nudism has nothing to do with the abolition of clothes. The humorists (?) who try to visualise a city of naked citizens; policemen and busmen without uniforms, city magnates and their typists devoid of clothing, and all the every-day population going about their daily business in a state of nakedness — have no thoughts in common with any Nudist. It is natural to remove clothing when it is desired to enjoy the full benefits of sun-bathing, or swimming, far more natural than to wear a bathing costume which prevents the beneficial rays from reaching the more important parts of the body and clings clammily to the body after immersion in the water. But no Nudist contemplates walking down a street or pursuing his business — in fact, appearing anywhere in public — without his clothes. It is true that in Germany a few years ago a large and important group of physical culturists gave a demonstration of nude-culture at a semi-public performance, but it may be taken for granted that the audience was a select one composed of interested supporters. There is nothing in common between a Nudist display of physical culture and the stage-shows featuring all-but nude dancing — and chorus girls accompanied by suggestive songs and salacious patter. No doubt there is plenty of good work for the "Purity League" in America to do in connection with such shows, but the distinction has already been made, and very forcibly too, by Miss Edith Neville, Chairman of the Stage Plays Committee, and Mr. Howard Tyrer, Secretary of the Public Morality Council, recently.* Sex itself is a natural phenomenon, but the artificial stimulation of sex instincts is the height of sophistication. The naturalness of Nudism is actually an effective antidote to sex stimulation, the anatomical differences between the sexes being taken as a matter of course and practically without significance. I have visited, with my wife, the principal Nudist clubs in this country, both outdoors and indoors, and never yet have either of us seen any untoward behaviour or anything to emphasise the sexual differences of our companions. Nor have I ever heard of any of my friends experiencing any unpleasantness which might arise from unusual incidents. I hope the actual experiences of myself and my friends will be admitted to be at least as convincing as any mere theory advanced by those lacking either experience or understanding. We lead such artificial lives nowadays that, without thought, we are apt to regard as unnatural some things which are the very essence of naturalness, and I think the shedding of clothes on suitable occasions is one of the most natural things a man (or woman) can do; only we have so far forgotten to be natural that we do not realise it.

What do Nudists do when they go to a camp or club and take off their clothes? Most of the men folk will take axe, or

* See *The Naked Truth about Nudism*: Subordination of Sex, pages 45 to 49.

chopper or spade, and join together in making or extending a clearing, cutting firewood or digging a cavity for the new swimming pool. If wire fences or hedges need attention, they will wear shorts or trousers and, perhaps, a sports shirt. They would not think of working in the nude where there was any possibility of being seen by the outside public. In one club of which I am a member a very substantial bridge was built from tree trunks, over which cars could run into the car park. Each worker on this job was dressed appropriately, and did not think of doffing his clothes until he was back in the sheltered clearing, where his nudity would be neither conspicuous nor offensive. Most members have huts or cabins or canvas tents. There is always work to be done on these. Carpentering, painting, roofing; new gadgets to be invented or constructed. Sometimes the women help in all these activities, but generally they confine themselves to cooking, washing up, house-cleaning and similar domestic pur-suits. All work and no play would make Jack a dull boy and scarcely prove attractive to Jill, so certain periods are devoted to games such as Badminton, Tenniquoit, Miniten and, in the more fortunate clubs, Lawn Tennis. What real enjoyment to play vigorous games entirely free from the hamper of clothing! Then there are round games in which all can join. A circle may be formed with one member in the centre, whom the other members try to hit, below the knees, with a football, the successful player taking his turn in the ring. Or one stands in the centre of the ring and throws, or pretends to throw, the ball to those standing round. No one must catch the ball without clapping his hands first, and if he claps his hands before the ball is thrown, he goes into the centre. These games may sound very simple in cold print, but they can be fast and quite exciting, while giving rise to more laughter than many a stage comedian. And all the time it is excellent exercise; hand, eye, brain, all parts of the body participating. Alternatively, the men can lie in a deck-chair or on the grass and read and smoke; the women can chat and knit, or sew or read too. And all the time there is a delightful sensation of complete freedom and relaxation. I know several individuals (of both sexes) who say that their first experience of a Nudist camp was the most enjoyable they had ever known. And why? Because it was all perfectly natural and what both body and mind need as an antidote to the artificial life led in the usual way.

I propose to deal with Fashion and its power over the public in my next chapter, and to show that it is as fickle as Fortune. No one can tell how freakish Fashion may prove at the next turn of the wheel, but many instances from the past may be considered in the light of evidence.

CHAPTER II

The Tyranny of Fashion

CLOTHES ARE MAINLY a question of Fashion, and Fashions may, like fire and water, be good servants but bad masters. Unfortunately, few fashions are founded on logic and commonsense, and many have proved definitely harmful to health. Fortunately, on the other hand, most fashions are comparatively short-lived. Nudism is not a fashion, although some people may think it is. Our primaeval ancestors lived without clothes; later ancestors, the Ancient Britons, relied for adornment chiefly on woad or a sort of blue staining or tattooing. Since then, all sorts of fashions have held sway. Although to-day clothes are supposed to be an essential of modesty, inasmuch as exposure of the body is considered immodest, it was not always so. So far as feminine fashions are concerned, they have nearly always been adopted as a means of exploiting sex. With the exception of a few years during the war, when an immature, almost boyish, outline was the ideal, the anatomical differences in sex have been emphasised by women's fashions. The hypocrisy of pretending that the nude body of a woman is immodest and likely to arouse lewd desires, and that it is covered up to avoid such wickedness, must be apparent after very little consideration. De Pomerai says in "Aphrodite": "Complete nakedness, as our savage forebears discovered thousands of years ago, is neither exciting nor sexually stimulating when familiar, its appeal being primarily to the aesthetic sense. But dress, or rather partial undress, adds a fictitious glamour to its wearer, concentrates attention upon the sexual characteristics which alone are concealed, stimulates the imagination and deliberately arouses desire." It has been said that the British nation is the most hypocritical nation in the world; but all civilised nations, in greater or lesser degree, are hypocritical regarding the covering of the body. It may be that women, conscious that their bodies are not naturally beautiful, have welcomed fashions which enabled them to appear more attractive physically than actually they were. Feminine fashions have always aimed at exposing, accentuating or simulating those features which have an essentially sexual significance. What are the main differences between the bodies of men and women? A woman's breasts, hips and gates, or buttocks, are probably the most salient features of her anatomy. In the interests of female modesty, one would think that these features would be made as unnoticeable as possible by the design of her clothing. But no! On the contrary, nearly all fashions have deliberately emphasised these essentially feminine attributes. In mediaeval times dresses were made of soft clinging stuff which was so moulded to the figure as to leave little or nothing to the imagination. The famous picture of Dante's first meeting with Beatrice displays the figure of Beatrice with as much frankness as if her torso, at least, were bare. Her breasts, nipples and navel are, as it were, thrust upon the eye by both costume and pose. Even the men of that period, with their tight-fitting hose (without the trunks of later date) wore little to disguise their masculinity. Yet these costumes were not considered immodest, because they were the *fashion* of the time. Later on, panniers were introduced to emphasise the breadth of women's hips. Ridiculously exaggerated and unnatural, of course, but the fundamental idea was unmistakable. Concurrently with this "showing off" in an artificial way of one part of the female anatomy came a greater exposure of flesh in the region of the shoulders and breasts. Eventually, this led to complete exposure of the breasts in very "fashionable" circles and all-but complete exposure as a general thing. The crinoline was just another example of "hip-exaggeration," and although this period was supposed to represent the acme of feminine modesty, the real origin of the fashion is indisputable. The fact that the majority of crinoline wearers failed to realise it does not invalidate the impeachment. With the crinoline came the exposure of the shoulders — quite a beautiful effect in its way, but surely not the apotheosis of modesty and sexual abnegation. Then the bustle — a monstrosity which had nothing to recommend it from the esthetic point of view and merely strove to call attention to that part of woman's anatomy which was at that time considered to be non-existent in polite conversation. In more recent years we had the "wasp-waist," formed by cruel and unhygienic corseting which compressed the waist and so accentuated the hips and the breasts, which it forced upwards and made more prominent. This fashion could hardly be claimed as an exemplification of modesty as assisted by clothing, but no doubt the people of the late Victorian or Edwardian era would have considered a Nudist camp or gymnasium positively disgusting.

Even in bathing costumes there have been fashions. I can remember the voluminous tunics with pleated skirts and deep collars, like small capes, bloomers and mob cap, all decorated with white or coloured braid. Uncomfortable, clumsy and unbecoming, they were worn because they were the fashion. Nobody thought of criticising them or pointing out the absurdity of such clothing for bathing. In America it was made compulsory to wear full-length stockings and long sleeves when frequenting public bathing beaches. How stupid all this must seem to the present generation! But it was accepted without comment in its day just because Dame Fashion decreed it. To-day a diminutive one-piece suit or slips and brassiere satisfy the demand for public decency; which is, at least, considerable progress towards commonsense and hygiene. It is not such a very great distance further to arrive at nude-bathing in sea, sun and air. Writing of the future of Nudism in *The Naked Truth about Nudism*, I said: "I see no reason why progressive seaside authorities should not set apart suitable coves or small bays for those who wish to bathe without costumes. Perhaps, at first, there might be separate sections for either sex, since the greatest objection seems to be the danger of observing the nudity of the opposite sex." Since I wrote that, I learned that nude sun-bathing (or, as they call it, "baking") is now allowed in Australia. The Melbourne *Argus* says: "The Coolangatta Town Council will permit sun-baking in the nude… The Town Clerk said to-day (28th September, 1936) that separate areas were being specially set apart for both males and females to sun-bake in the nude." And, according to a correspondent in the *Sun-bathing Review*, the Town Clerk of Paignton in our own England has announced that children may bathe and play on the beach there in complete nudity.

One fact which becomes obvious on consideration of the foregoing is that the question of clothing is, as I said at the beginning of this chapter, a matter of Fashion. If a change in Fashion should make nudity the correct thing on our seaside beaches (which I think very unlikely), a person wearing a bathing costume would at once appear "unnatural" and for once the criticism would be perfectly true. While we must all agree that a certain amount of convention is necessary for the smooth and satisfactory conduct of our social life, there seems to be no good reason why the conventions should not be founded on commonsense. I am afraid very few of them are, particularly as regards clothing. One thing which ladies should remember, when considering this subject, is that modern fashions are much more sensible and comfortable for women than they are for men. Women do not have to wear high, stiff and tight collars round their necks. Their arms and necks, and often a good proportion of their chests, are free even in what may be called their full dress. Compare a soft, flowing evening gown, cut low either in front or behind, or both, with the starched collar and shirt and tight-fitting coat of a man in evening dress! The woman, cool and comfortable, glories in this phase of Fashion because, if she has taste and money, it enables her to be seen to the greatest advantage. The man puts up with it because he dreads the social obloquy which ignorance or defiance of the standard would bring. A great many men, used to donning this uncomfortable and unbecoming costume, will tell you that they are quite happy in it and enjoy wearing it. But how many would care to adopt it for sport or recreation or those occasions on which they desire to relax? I think that is one of the weaknesses of the — in many ways admirable — public school training. The real object of these schools is to turn out a "type." People say of a man, "A typical public schoolboy." It means that he may be safely relied upon to conform to the fashion of the public school of his day. His individuality must suffer, some of the habits he acquires may not be wholly admirable, but he is cast in the mould, and the degree of success attained by his preceptors is largely judged by this almost slavish loyalty to the form set as a standard. It is possible that many a striking individuality has been sacrificed on this Moloch-like altar of fashion and convention.

Again let me remind you that fashions are ephemeral. To-day it is absolutely vital, from the Fashion point of view, that you should dress like this and like that. Tomorrow you will be scorned and contemned if you have not changed to something quite different. The Nudist, while he is practising Nudism, is untrammelled by these arbitrary decrees. The fashion of a Nudist is a sound, well-shaped body without any extraneous adornment. And this fashion can never change. Broad shoulders, narrow hips, well-developed muscles in arms, legs and torso will never be ousted by a desire for bottle-shoulders and puny limbs.

In a woman, soft curves, firm, well-developed breasts and pliant carriage will never be *demode*. Why should we give way to the tyranny of this false Goddess "Fashion"? Often enough a fashion is changed as a commercial "stunt" — to ensure that people will buy more new clothes and so enrich the coffers of those parasitic industries which hide behind the Goddess as the priests of Moloch hid behind their god. I do not suggest that we should make ourselves conspicuous by eccentricities in dress, but let us be as natural as we can. Let us wear clothes that are comfortable and hygienic as well as pleasing to the eye. And whenever possible, let us wear no clothes at all. Not in public, of course, but on those occasions when we want to be very vigorous or very much at ease.

When one thinks of Fashion, one usually thinks of styles in women's dress. But men's fashions change too. In my time there has been a change from very tight trousers to very wide ones. "Oxford Bags" was a fashion of a day, although it has left its impress upon subsequent styles. Starched collars, three inches in height, have given place to lower collars and soft or "semi-soft" materials. The soft felt hat or "Trilby," as it was first called, is now almost universal; yet it had to survive a period of ridicule and derision when first introduced. Perhaps the gayest and most picturesque period of fashion was during the Restoration. Rich materials, a great deal of labour and a certain freedom in colouring were involved. The Cavalier enjoyed almost as much scope in personal adornment as his lady. The Georgian beaux could also be proud of the appearance they made with knee breeches, full-bottomed coats and flowered waistcoats. But there is little upon which the man of to-day can congratulate himself. How much better, how much more natural, if man (and woman, too) would pay less attention to Fashion's vagaries and concentrate on improving the body itself!

There was one period, perhaps, when we could say that a beautiful body was "fashionable" — during the Greek supremacy. In those days the body was considered before clothes, with the result that the highest compliment that can be paid to a young man to-day is that he looks like "a Greek god" or a young woman as "a Greek goddess." Nobody ever

forgotten that once the human body was admired for itself, for the health and strength and suppleness which it signified. The latest style of hat or coat is eagerly sought after; the body remains neglected or regarded at best as a peg upon which to hang expensive garments. The ancient gods Moloch, Baal, Momus, Ate and Pluto have been dethroned for centuries, but the Goddess Fashion still holds sway, and until we all spend a little more time and energy in thought, she will continue to be exploited for purely commercial ends. Primitive races, which we are apt to regard with good-humoured contempt, have their fashions, but they usually conform to the laws of Nature and in no way impede physical perfection. With them, health and strength, manual dexterity and courage are fostered and regarded with the respect and admiration which they merit. Nudists do not desire to make physical excellence their sole aim. Usually they are intelligent, thoughtful people whose brains are quite as well developed as their muscles, but the "joy of living" appeals to them as an integral part of life and they find the practice of Nudism of benefit to body and mind alike.

Since fashions in the past have made no secret of woman's anatomy, as has been shown, we should not give undue weight to the idea that lack of clothes necessitates impropriety. So far as health and happiness are concerned, I hope to show in Chapter IV that the body is better off without any clothing at all — at least on occasions.

CHAPTER III

"Back to Nature"

SOME CRITICS OF Nudism are apt to confuse it with various "Back to Nature" movements. Professor Low, a little while ago, said: "To me, Nudism, Naturism, and back to the land, or back to anywhere else, are all wrong." He even went so far as to suggest that we should "train our bodies into atrophy" and look forward to the time when "the all-brain jelly man and woman of the future will satisfy all needs by thought." I wrote an article in reply to Professor Low's, in which I pointed out that our physical fitness has a very important bearing upon our intellectual and moral fitness. That although science and progress, in certain forms, have taught us how to provide substitutes for natural foods, laws had been found necessary to check deleterious adulterations, and that there was no logic in using artificially produced ultra-violet and infra-red rays when natural sunshine was available. Nudism is not based upon "going back" to anything. We may say that it is desirable not to lose contact with Nature; not to forget nor overlook those essentials of Nature without which we can be neither healthy nor happy. Professor Low's contention that we want "Motor cars, not legs. Television and glasses, not eyes," is not likely, I think, to meet with general agreement. On the other hand, it is quite wrong to believe that Nudists desire to revert to a state of savagery and primitive asceticism. All sorts of individuals may be found in the Nudist ranks.

Vegetarians, non-smokers, teetotallers, Nonconformists, Socialists, Theosophists; some who disbelieve in capital punishment or vivisection. But none of these sectarians represent Nudism as a whole any more than they represent the British nation, or the Conservative Party or the Church of England. They may be found in all walks of life. Amongst the Nudists known to me personally are successful businessmen, Government servants, clergymen, solicitors and scientists. To be a Nudist means no more than to be an Englishman.

Let us examine this "Back to Nature" fallacy. Do Nudists live upon uncooked foods which they have secured by their own hands, as primitive man is supposed to have done? The answer is definitely negative. Do they earn their livings by tilling the ground or hunting and fishing? They do not. They work and live just as other law-abiding intelligent people do, and in their own homes they may have electric light, radiograms, and, perhaps, an excellent library. To them a Nudist camp is a place where they can feel free for a few hours to bask in the sun or restore their vitality with vigorous exercise and fresh air. The simplicity of camp life is a pleasant reaction from the stuffiness and turmoil of the daily routine. The opportunity of airing the body, stretching the muscles and being, for a while, perfectly natural. Many of the most progressive minds are attracted by the amenities offered. I think we are inclined to over-value the advantages brought by civilisation and so-called progress. Health services, such as efficient drainage and hospitals, provided by civilisation are largely the outcome of necessities caused by this same civilisation. If progress puts more motor cars on the roads, we must have more hospitals to care for the increasing numbers of those injured by motor cars. The conditions in overcrowded towns are so inimical to health that special precautions must be taken to preserve, as far as may be, a general standard of health. Usually this standard is not a very high one. Wonderful things have been done in the design and manufacture of artificial limbs, eye-glasses and spectacles. Those who have need of their artificial aid may well be grateful to science and industry; but it would be far better if more natural living made them unnecessary. Primitive races get along quite well without them. I know that, in this country, it is impracticable to try and live a perfectly natural life. After generations of unnatural living I do not think we could stand up to a really primitive existence; and I am quite sure very few of us would like it. But we can make a compromise, and Nudism offers a practical and pleasant compromise. Whole-wheat and rye biscuits and bread are advertised daily; most cereal foods and non-alcoholic beverages are recommended for their health-giving qualities, and the consumption throughout the country must be very considerable; yet the consumers are not regarded as cranks and derided as "Back to Naturists." To believe in Nudism and to practise it on suitable occasions does not necessitate complete renunciation of material comforts and social amenities. I like comfort and convenience; I have a radiogram, electric light, telephone and a car; I am far, I hope, from being a savage, and quite content to abide by reasonable conventions. Perhaps you will say it is inconsistent to own and use these things if I believe in Nudism. I might reply that it is far more inconsistent for you to eat, drink and do things which are not good for you and make no attempt to rectify matters except by taking patent medicines or nostrums which claim to cure indigestion, constipation, colds and headaches. Or you may eat and drink food and beverages which you believe will benefit your health. Very well, I practise Nudism because I believe it benefits my health, and I possess very good evidence to prove that it does. Quite apart from the health question, I derive a great deal of pleasure from it. If you never have felt the sun soaking into your bare skin all over your body, or played games with the freedom which only nudity can give, it will be almost impossible for you to realise just how enjoyable it can be. Or even to run about in the rain or stand under a tree while someone shakes the drops off the leaves on to your bare body; it is totally different from an ordinary shower-bath. I have seen children, my own among them, dancing about in the rain, and when it had stopped, following a young man from tree to tree to have the drops shaken on them.

This is certainly getting back to Nature, in a sense; and lying in the sun or a shady nook with the body completely exposed to soft breezes, causes one to meditate on the beauties of Nature more than so-called sun-bathing in a woolly costume on a noisy and crowded beach. Even social contacts seem more natural under these conditions. Newcomers seem to feel at home almost immediately and to throw off minor discontents with their garments. On one occasion last summer I was very busy creosoting our but and crouching on the ground in my "birthday suit," when I heard the voice of one of my friends say, "I want you to meet ___ and ___." I looked up, and there were two young ladies, fully dressed, whom he had invited to visit the Club. Nude, crouched on the ground and probably spotted with creosote, I felt not the slightest embarrassment, nor, apparently, did they. We chatted for a few moments, and then they moved off to be introduced to other members, and I got on with my job. With my two boys, I have cut down small trees and built a kind of pergola in front of the hut, which will be roofed with either canvas or bracken before next summer, and this gives a sensation of getting back to Nature and primitive home-building. I find it delightful, and I believe most people would because we all retain a certain instinctive desire to build nests or raise up protection with our own hands for ourselves and our families. Nevertheless, I read a lot, listen to the "wireless" talks on world affairs, go to cinemas and theatres, and enjoy an intelligent discussion. I have taken part in some most interesting talks round a camp fire and listened to accounts of travels and adventures of other members in an indoor Nudist club. I can appreciate a good dinner at a smart West-End restaurant, but I get as much, or more, enjoyment from the aroma of bacon and sausages sizzling over a wood fire at camp. And the smell of the woods in the early morning, after a night of showers, is something to be remembered.

I do not think I should like to spend the whole of my life, winter and summer, year after year, in a Nudist camp, and there are times when I appreciate the comfort of the big woolly ulster which I wear sometimes for motoring. It is the change or the contrast which makes so many things enjoyable, and the knowledge that one is improving one's health at the same time is an additional gratification. Some of my friends work and play nude in the snow. I have never yet tried that, but I hope to someday. I have found that it is often warmer to be entirely without clothes than to wear a little. In sunshine this is obvious, because the warmth of the sun can reach the skin without being filtered through the clothing; but even out of the sun the skin will work more efficiently when bare.

Then there is diet. The only member of my family who is a vegetarian is my small daughter, who eschews meat, not from conviction, but because she just does not like meat. I did not myself as a child, and I eat very little now. At camp, simple food is general. There are no facilities for elaborate cooking, and fruits and salads seem most suitable as summer fare. But we do not "go back to Nature" so far as to eat with our fingers, or gnaw bones, or ignore the use of soap and water. We have washing bowls, brushes and combs, and safety razors. We sleep on beds (except the children) and use woollen blankets and sleeping bags. We even have oil and spirit stoves for emergency. So you see it is quite possible to live a fairly natural and healthy life without degenerating into savagery.

In *The Future of Nakedness*, Professor Parmalee says: "The new gymnosophy endeavours… to regain what mankind has lost through civilisation, without rejecting anything of human, social and cultural value." I think "Gymnosophy" a rather pretentious name for Nudism, but his statement is a very clear and truthful description of our aims. Incidentally, I wonder how many people realise that the word "gymnasium" is derived from the Greek "Gymnos," which means "naked" and refers to the places, indoors and out, where the Greeks used to practise physical culture in the nude! Possibly some parents would be shocked to think that schools where their children were being educated possessed "nakedness-halls."

There have been some rather eccentric people who have advocated an absolute return to Nature; such as the young officer and his wife, who, a few years ago, decided to spend their three months' honeymoon in a forest without any of the supports of civilisation. No matches, no tools, no weapons.

I am not quite sure how they reckoned to live; possibly on wild fruits and edible fungi, if their botanical knowledge was equal to it. They were not Nudists, and although they were prepared to abandon almost all other civilised attributes, they did not propose to go entirely without clothes. I think this was rather more foolish than the way in which some people spend their summer holidays at the seaside — burning their skins in the endeavour to get brown quickly, keeping late hours, over-eating, exhausting themselves with unaccustomed exercise one day, and taking none at all the next. There is certainly something in what foreigners say about the English not knowing how to enjoy themselves. Nudists know, and the novices soon learn from the more experienced, that irradiation, diet and exercises require understanding and adjusting to individual requirements. To live naturally, one must be in harmony with Nature; prefer simple foods and fresh air to excitement and artificial stimulants. Even if such conditions are enjoyed only occasionally, at weekends, or on daily trips, they make a complete change from the trying life which most of us lead, and act as a restorative of our jaded faculties. There is a deal of satisfaction, too, in the wielding of an axe or spade; especially when one acquires a certain amount of dexterity in their use; the sense of achievement when a task is accomplished, the vigorous circulation of the blood and tension of the muscles. Physical exertion ensures, automatically, the filling of the lungs with oxygen and the displacement of the poisonous carbon-dioxide. Few of us would care to give up, permanently, the comforts and conveniences to which we have grown used, but the temporary throwing off of the shackles of convention is refreshing to both body and spirit.

Nor are Nudists contemptuous of comfort even in camp. Many little gadgets are improvised to make life easier and more enjoyable, and there is a lot of fun to be gained from such activities. Vanity, even, may be indulged, to a moderate extent, by the accessories which you can provide by use of your own brains and hands. I spent a lot of thought in designing and making the fittings of our hut — shelves, towel rails, clothes hangers, and a capacious locker, the top of which serves as a seat. We have a colour scheme, too. The sides and back are creosoted (eventually they will be treated with a mixture of creosote and coal tar); the front is painted white with green doors, and the inside is a combination of primrose and soft powder blue, which gives an excellent effect of sunshine and blue sky. Would you consider this barbaric or atavistic? Does it suggest that we have fallen to the level of ignorant savages or are eccentric cranks without appreciation of the good things of life?

Two Nudist friends of mine have, between them, designed and constructed one of those diminutive aeroplanes popularly known as a "Flying Flea." One of them is a Professor at a well-known University. Another Nudist I know is a Director of a big engineering and electrical undertaking, who has, I believe, been responsible for several useful inventions. Do you think it odd that men of indubitable brainpower should enjoy the occasional freedom of a Nudist community? It is not, really. Some of our great men go big-game shooting abroad under very primitive conditions; it renews their physical and mental vitality, so that they can come back and do even bigger things. The average man looks forward to his annual holiday at the seaside or in the country, when he can change his everyday wear for open-necked shirts and, perhaps, shorts or loose flannel trousers, and be a little more natural than he dare be in his everyday life. And he comes back refreshed and re-energised to carry on for another fifty weeks of monotonous routine. He would benefit still more if he followed the example of those who give their skins the opportunity of storing up sunshine vitamins for reserves during the sunless days ahead until the next summer holiday.

Perhaps it is difficult for the non-Nudist to realise how a certain amount of nature-life can be enjoyed without sacrificing the good features of modern civilised life. I had rather a shock on one occasion when keeping an appointment with the chief technical officer of a very big organisation to investigate the merits of infra-red apparatus heated by gas. He looked at me for a few seconds, and said: Well, Mr. Welby, I *am* disappointed!" I asked what he was disappointed about, and he said that he at least expected me to appear in an open-necked shirt and shorts, and probably sandals. I was sorry to disappoint him, but I keep my naturalistic and my business activities in separate compartments without any urge to mix them or any fear of them clashing. It seems almost impossible for some people to refrain from mixing their politics or religion with their business and social life, but Nudists never obtrude their opinions in general conversation; nor is there anything about their behaviour which would make them conspicuous in ordinary company.

I have mentioned in one of my books how I met at the National Nudist Conference an acquaintance whom I had thought might be shocked at the thought of my writing a book on Nudism, and then discovered that he had been a member of a Nudist Club for nearly a year. In another instance, a friend of mine was wondering how he could approach his brother on the subject without shocking him, when I recognised the brother as a member of another Nudist Club, of which my wife and I were members. So, you see, there is no "brand of Cain" or obvious peculiarity to stamp the Nudist as in any way different from his fellow men. Nudism means not "going back to Nature" in the freakish sense, but a realisation of the need for retaining sufficient contact with the essentials of a healthy body and appreciation of the pleasures to be enjoyed when living in harmony with Nature instead of in a state of enmity or indifference. Just what those essentials are may be considered in our next chapter, "Nature's Needs."

CHAPTER IV

Nature's Needs

THE HUMAN BODY is like a chemical factory or rather like a chain of factories linked together and supporting one another, similar to Henry Ford's factories in America. To carry on their work these factories need fuel and raw materials. Food provides the fuel (estimated in calories or heat units) and the raw materials to be manufactured into different substances. This changing of the food is called metabolism, which refers to two distinctive processes — anabolism, or building up into more elaborate substances; and katabolism, or breaking down into simpler substances. The raw materials needed are many and varied; amongst them are animal fats such as butter, cream, dripping, lard and suet; vegetable fats such as olive oil, almond oil, and oil obtained from cocoanuts and soya beans. There are also fish oils like cod-liver oil and halibut-liver oil. Then there are carbohydrates, mainly sugars and starches and mineral salts. The latter include lime, iron, copper, magnesium, calcium, phosphorus, iodine and sodium, one of the most important being sodium chloride or common salt. The common gateway of our factories is the mouth, where the goods are received, chewed, and mixed with saliva so that they will pass easily down the oesophagus, or gullet, to the stomach. This is a sort of store-house, whence the food (in a partially digested state) is passed on to the intestines, which complete the digestion and act as a distributing organisation. The real chemical factories are the liver, kidneys, pancreas, and various glands. Here the raw material received by the mouth is transformed and eventually formed into living tissue — skin, flesh, bone, hair, teeth and nails.

All this is very wonderful and not yet completely understood even by our scientists; the main point is that Nature cannot carry on her work without the right kind and quantity of raw materials and the proper conditions. More often than not, we fail to supply our factories with the right materials and conditions, otherwise we would never be ill. We eat too much of one thing and not enough of another, or we have too little exercise or too little sleep. To burn up the carbon and purify our blood, our lungs must be well supplied with oxygen, which means deep breathing in fresh air and suitable muscular exercises. We all know that we cannot live without breathing, but how many of us really know how to breathe and take its practice seriously? Only deep and regular breathing can eliminate the carbon dioxide from all the cells in our lungs and refill them with oxygen. And if we do not eliminate all the carbon dioxide, we are allowing the blood to carry this poison to all parts of our body, for to continue our analogy, the blood is the transport system of our factories and conveys their finished products to what we may call the consumers.

Again, exercise is needed to circulate the blood. It is no use our ignoring the needs of Nature, because she neither will nor can carry out her duties unless she is assisted or at least unhindered. All systems of physical culture are directed to those ends; proper breathing, circulation of the blood, correct diet and elimination of waste and poisonous matter. One would think there could be no subject or object so absorbingly interesting and so vitally important. Athletes do study these things; they have to if they wish to be successful, but we cannot all be athletes. Just to live happily and healthily is enough for most of us, and to do this we must give consideration to the facts and abide by the rules.

Now how does Nudism help us to do this? In many ways. If we are sincere Nudists and join a properly organised community, we shall find more opportunities and more encouragement to enjoy fresh air and exercise. Whether the exercising is in the form of scientifically prepared courses, games, or in camp work, we shall be sure of it, and in the fresh air, too. One can rest and relax part of the time, but the need and incentive to exercise will always be at hand. The mere force of example will cause many a lax and indolent individual to become more active, and once the benefit is realised, it will be continued for its own sake. I have seen some remarkable transformations effected in those who have taken up the practice. I used to be quite keen on physical exercises when a youth; I had dumb-bells and a "Sandow Developer," but for a great many years I had hardly any exercise at all until I became a Nudist. There are a few people who possess the moral courage to "do their daily dozen" at home and in solitude, but they are very much in the minority; the majority need some sort of moral support, and this is provided in a Nudist community. The spark of vanity which, in greater or lesser degree, burns in all of us, is another influence for good. With nothing in the way of clothes to adorn us or cover up our imperfections, the need for improving and maintaining a reasonably fit body becomes obvious and urgent. Nudists are not in the habit of staring at one another with aggressive criticism, but deep down in our subconscious we feel a desire to appear to as much advantage as possible and a definite pride of body is developed. Membership of a tennis, cricket or golf club will not — cannot — exert quite the same influence, nor give rise to the same needs. So much for exercise and fresh air.

There is much more than this to be considered, however. Amongst the organs mentioned above I purposely omitted reference to the skin. So important is this in connection with the subject that it requires separate consideration. The skin is more than a mere covering to our flesh. It is an active organ with specific duties to perform, just like the heart, liver, kidneys and other organs. It is in fact another chemical factory. It is the main factor in controlling the temperature of our bodies — a very important function. Sudden chills or overheating are extremely dangerous, and often the cause of serious illnesses. And to do this efficiently it must be kept in proper condition by being exercised as the muscles are exercised. If we keep our skin constantly covered up and rely upon clothes to control our body temperature, its efficiency will be weakened just as muscles are weakened if they are not used. While sudden chills must be avoided, it is good for the skin to be subjected to changes of temperature. A warm bath with a cold or tepid shower invigorates and braces the nerves and tones up the skin generally. Cold air on the surface of the skin while the body is warmed up by vigorous exercise and circulation of the blood is extremely beneficial. When the pores are opened by heat, there is greater facility for exuding poisonous and waste matter. The kidneys are mainly responsible for this in the ordinary way, but too much work for them may overtax them and lead to inefficient elimination.

There are four organs provided for this purpose: the kidneys, the bowels, the lungs and the skin. If the latter is not allowed to do its work properly, an undue demand is made upon the other three organs, with the possibility of a breakdown in the system. The skin contains a multitude of tiny glands known as sebaceous glands and sweat glands. The former secrete an oily fluid for the lubrication of the hair and skin; the latter are formed of little tubes deep down in the layers of skin connected to the surface by another tube with four holes or openings. These sweat glands contain water carried to them by the bloodstream (which contains about 80 per cent of water) and they "trap" certain poisons and waste products which need to be worked out of the system. The word "perspire" is derived from the Latin and means, literally, "to breathe everywhere," so that the need for the skin to be unhindered in this process is obvious. The amount of fluid absorbed by these glands mainly depends upon the quantity of blood circulating in the skin and whether it is drawn near the surface by heat, or repelled by cold, which causes the blood-vessels to contract and so offer less blood for cooling. The fact that the average man evaporates in perspiration over a pint a day is evidence of the importance of this function. About 99 per cent of the fluid consists of water, the other I per cent being made up from the waste or "ashes" of the protein and certain salts, such as chlorides and phosphates.

Perspiration is effective, mostly, in the form of vapour, which is invisible and is known as "insensible" perspiration.

liable to decomposition, the need for constant changes of clothing is apparent. And unless the clothing is changed at very frequent periods, almost hourly, we must carry these waste products about with us. With regular and frequent ablutions and changing of underwear, this is not a very serious matter but consider how much easier and how much better it must be if the skin is allowed to carry out its work naturally, without the handicap of clothes. Sunlight, real or artificial, is a very potent bacteriacide, and germs lodged in the skin can be completely destroyed by direct exposure to the ultra-violet rays. While the skin is covered with clothing which these rays cannot penetrate, the bacteria are at liberty to increase and multiply without let or hindrance… and undoubtedly do.

Before leaving our consideration of Nature's Needs, there is another vital factor which should be understood and remembered. In addition to the raw materials for our internal factories, referred to at the beginning of this Chapter, fats, carbohydrates and mineral salts, there are certain essential substances known as Vitamins. The existence of these vitamins was discovered by Sir Gowland Hopkins and made known by him in 1912. Those most important and generally understood are Vitamins A, B, C and D. Although they are not, in themselves, nutritive, they are vital constituents in the process of metabolism, and were they absent from the system, life would cease. Insufficiency in any one of them will cause a breakdown of the internal economy.

Calcium has been mentioned as one of the essential "raw materials," but though calcium may be taken, it will not be properly absorbed and made into bone, teeth and other tissues unless accompanied by the necessary Vitamin D.

Lack of calcium and Vitamin D is responsible for the disease "rickets," unfortunately still prevalent among children. This can be treated successfully by ultra-violet rays and foods known to be rich in Vitamin D. This vitamin has been called the "Sunshine" vitamin, and here we come to another very important reason for exposing the whole of the body to the sun. The skin possesses the ability, when subjected to irradiation, of forming and storing up Vitamin D. Those who enjoy a good sunbathing season during the summer can reasonably face a bad winter with a certain amount of confidence. I used to be subject to very bad influenza colds, but since I took up sun-bathing and installed a "sunshine lamp" in my bedroom (I now have two, a "Hanovia Homesun" and a "Quain") I have been practically immune.

In considering Nature's Needs, therefore, I think we may fairly regard exposure of the body to sun and air as one of the necessities. Partial exposure, by wearing a bathing costume or shorts, may be good; but complete exposure must surely be better. At various institutions — Dr. Rollier's at Leysin in Switzerland, and Sir Henry Gauvrain's at Alton and Hayling Island — many ailments have been cured or alleviated by sunlight treatment. Credit for the original discovery of the therapeutic value of sunlight should probably be given to Finsen. Notwithstanding the fact that the Greeks and Romans took "sun-cures" in ancient times, Finsen was the first man with scientific training to study the subject and put it on a practical basis. In 1885, when he was a medical student, Finsen is said to have watched a cat on a neighbouring roof. As the transit of the sun moved the shadow of the house overlooking this roof, so the cat moved in order to remain in the sun, and the result of Finsen's observations was that he studied the light rays to such good purpose that he became famous as a "helio-therapist" or "light-doctor." He has been followed by many others, and his theories have been tested and proved of incalculable value. In hospitals where natural sunlight is unavailable, or insufficient, powerful lamps are installed which emit the ultra-violet and infra-red rays, and similar lamps of lesser power may be obtained for home use.

I hope I have made it clear in the foregoing pages that Nudism is definitely an aid to health and in accord with Nature's Needs; but I believe that spiritually and mentally or psychologically, as you will, it is no less valuable. I have called my next chapter "Body and Soul," because in it I shall try to show how the two are linked together and are equally benefited by the practice of Nudism with reasonable discrimination.

CHAPTER V

Body and Soul

COMPLEX AS THE body is, it is far easier to understand than the mind. The science of psychology, or study of the mind, gives us a good deal of knowledge, however, and it is known that conditions of body and mind have definite effects upon each other. That Nudism is good for bodily health is fairly generally admitted now, and the facts I have given in the previous chapter speak for themselves. There are other factors which merit equal consideration. I, like so many other people, was attracted to the movement solely on account of the health factor, but I have come to see that the psychological side of Nudism deserves far more credit than hitherto it has received.

On my very first visit to a Nudist Club, the secretary suggested that I had made the physical advantages of Nudism very clear in *Naked and Unashamed*, but had scarcely done justice to the social aspect. That started me thinking, and I was thereafter alert to observe and weigh evidence in this direction. I found plenty. As a family we had been rather self-centred and not very keen on making acquaintances. I would not say that our minds and our sympathies were therefore narrow, but on looking back over the past three years, I can see how our associations with Nudists have broadened them. We have not only met more people; we have met more types of people, because although all Nudists have much in common, they are mostly rather "out of the rut." This is only natural. Men and women with little experience of life and of phlegmatic temperament are less likely to be attracted by what may seem, on first thought, so revolutionary an idea as to mix socially in a state of nudity. The more adventurous and active types, those who have travelled and observed conditions in other parts of the world, are far more ready to accept new notions and adapt themselves more easily. In one club I heard a member describing the life of the natives in some wild part of Africa, when a man sitting near joined in the conversation and amplified the first speaker's explanation of certain technicalities with some first-hand experiences of his own in the same district. Another man told me how he had joined the Army at the age of 14, was sent to India, where he served for some years — he remembered Quetta when it consisted mainly of native huts — and then served with the British Army in Egypt. Subsequently, he transferred to the native camel corps, in which he lived like an Arab; and after this he took charge of a trading station on the West Coast of Africa. We were friendly with a man and his wife for some time before we learned that they had met, and become engaged in the Fiji Islands, where she was a hospital nurse and he owned a sugar plantation. While we were discussing motor cars, he told me that he had driven in each one of the Continents — Europe, America, Australia, Africa and Asia. An Australian told me that, with his brothers and sisters, he swam and sun-bathed in the nude regularly when they were all youngsters, and that he had practised Nudism many years ago in Australasia, Polynesia and America. He was a fine specimen of manhood at 60, and did not look more than a well-preserved 50.

I could give many more instances and refer to the letters I have received from almost every corner of the World, but I think sufficient has been said to show that one may meet interesting and widely experienced people in Nudist communities. This in itself is good for the mind. Contact with alert intelligences and vigorous minds broadened by travel is a form of education and recreation combined. It refreshes us mentally and spiritually while our bodies are being invigorated. The sort of conversation that occurs during these gatherings is usually more intellectual than is found at whist drives or the average golf or tennis club. There is a kind of Freemasonry, too, which ensures a kindliness and thoughtfulness for each other and a readiness to share food or possessions. When we first camped out, I did not feel very keen on going out into the wet to make a fire and boil a kettle for our early tea; but one member, with a hut and an oil stove, boiled water and took it round to everyone who wanted it. Socially, one is likely to find greater inducement to make and meet friends under such conditions. To the uninitiated, a Nudist Club might seem the most unlikely place to meet people who are what is usually termed "shy." Yet I have met many who might be virtually "tongue-tied" in ordinary society and have found them ready to talk on various subjects with an intelligence and understanding which would surprise those who had seen them only in conventional situations. There is a reason for this. Most of us labour under unconscious repressions and inhibitions which prevent us from really being ourselves. From childhood we have been hedged in with a code which said we must not do that and we must do this, without any satisfactory reason being given to us, until we have formed a sort of artificial shell about our true selves. The casting off of our clothes is a symbol of emancipation. Without realising it, we feel a shattering of shackles and fetters, and return in some sense to the psychological freedom of our early childhood.

Apart from any question of Nudism, the throwing off of clothes inculcates in all of us a sense of relief. The labourer, after his day of hard manual work, sheds his coat and waistcoat and boots with the idea of feeling at ease. The "black-coated worker" may change into a sports shirt and flannel trousers or loose sports jacket. The man and woman of a higher social sphere, with evening engagements probably, will wait until a later hour, when they don dressing gown or negligee for a spell of freedom before going to bed. Primarily these changes are made with a view to physical comfort, but there is also the subconscious urge to be free from the iron-bound conventions of the outside world. On holidays a minimum of clothing is part of the holiday enjoyment, and again shorts and bathing costumes serve only partly for physical comfort; the spiritual ease is at least as important. When do we start our holidays? When we enter the train which is to bear us to the sea or country and away from the everyday routine for a spell. Often the physical comfort is far to seek in a stuffy, crowded railway carriage; but we are "on holiday" and the spirit of freedom has entered into us. This spiritual freedom is intensified in the practice of Nudism to a degree difficult for the non-Nudist to appreciate. The difference between changing into lighter and more comfortable clothing and changing into no clothes at all is as great as the difference between a prison cell and the wide open spaces. In suitable weather one experiences a form of exhilaration comparable with the inhalation of sea breezes. As the last garment is dispensed with, one feels almost buoyant and ready for work or play with a quite unusual zest. In exercising or playing vigorous games even in the minimum of clothing — say, shorts and vest — there is always some slight feeling of restriction which is entirely obviated when in the nude.

Freud suggests that we all suffer from "guilt-complexes" mainly concerned with sex repressions. Possibly we all desire the freedom of nakedness, but are inhibited by a sense of guilt on exposing the whole of our bodies. This is really quite unwarranted, and when we are in the society of a number of other naked people, of both sexes, all unselfconscious and at ease, the burden of this inhibition is lifted and we become spiritually free.

Although I have always felt that Freudian philosophy over-emphasised the sexual significance of our psychological maladjustments, I do believe that many forms of neurosis are caused by ignorance or misunderstanding of sex. In early child-hood, sex has no significance whatever, except in abnormal cases; in adolescence it is usually a very disturbing factor; and in the adult, the results of adolescent disturbances may take unexpected shape. Sexual perversions, neurasthenia, impotency and misanthropy may be brought about through complexes formed during adolescence. Secrecy and mystery are the forerunner of curiosity and pruriency, and are responsible for an artificial interest in the sexual regions of the opposite sex. I have met several men who have asserted that the sight of a nude female would cause an immediate physical reaction of an embarrassing nature, at least in themselves. I do not believe this. I regard it as an unnatural and unhealthy attitude of mind which would be entirely dissipated by association with a Nudist group. Children and young people who grow up in familiarity with nudity could have no such feeling or ideas. The idea that the unclothed body is suggestive of lewdness or eroticism is the result of ignorance and false teaching. It is on a par with the whisperings and sniggerings of schoolboys and unintelligent youths when discussing matters of sex; themselves, perhaps, the product of generations of hypocrisy and misinformation. In a Nudist community there is no ground for curiosity. The frank exposure of the body, as a matter of course, disposes of all conjecture and speculation, such as may be induced by clothes which accentuate and partially reveal sexual characteristics.

Many of the clergy and moral reformers have denounced the semi-nudity of the stage and the cinema. I think they have a very good case, because the atmosphere of indoor places of entertainment like these is one of unnatural stimulation of all the senses; there is an artificial glamour and romance thrown over erotic and, perhaps, immoral situations. The costumes — what there is of them — are usually suggestive and lead thought into unwholesome channels.

The conditions in a genuine Nudist Club are quite different. Instead of super-induced emotionalism, one finds a soothing and freshening influence amid natural surroundings. Nothing being concealed, there is nothing to excite the imagination, and the lack of self-consciousness in one's companions disperses self-consciousness in each individual. There is nothing to hide, nothing to wonder about, nothing to induce what someone has described as "a delicious sense of guilt." With the intelligence and experience of maturity the average Nudist has the mind of a child so far as nudity is concerned. Then there is no class distinction in the way of dress. Appearance is no indication of financial or social standing. Those to be most admired are those who possess the healthiest and most beautiful bodies, not those who can afford the most expensive clothes. Everyone is accepted on his own merits; behaviour, speech and general companionability are the touchstones. Good breeding and true gentility do not, or should not, need uniforms or badges to indicate their existence. Imagine the difference, on a smoking hot day, between complete nudity and the restriction of formal clothes such as are worn in business or social occasions! It is true that ladies have far more licence in this respect than men, but even a light summer frock, with its accompanying underwear, may become irksome by comparison. Nearly all the newcomers I have known have remarked their feeling of distaste when having to "dress-up" to go home. They just hate having to put on their clothes again.

While Nudism is really only intended for temporary relaxation on suitable occasions, I know many enthusiasts who discard their clothes at home whenever practicable. Some have "sun-bathing shelters" in their own gardens so that they may take every opportunity of giving their bodies an air- or sun-bath. And, let me repeat, this is not done for physical reasons alone; it actually lightens the burden of their cares and imparts a "holiday-feeling."

I sincerely believe there is more light-heartedness to be found in a Nudist community than in any other form of social reunion. I would not even except the cocktail parties of Bright Young Things, because I think these are not due so much to natural spirits as to spirits out of a bottle and the desire (not

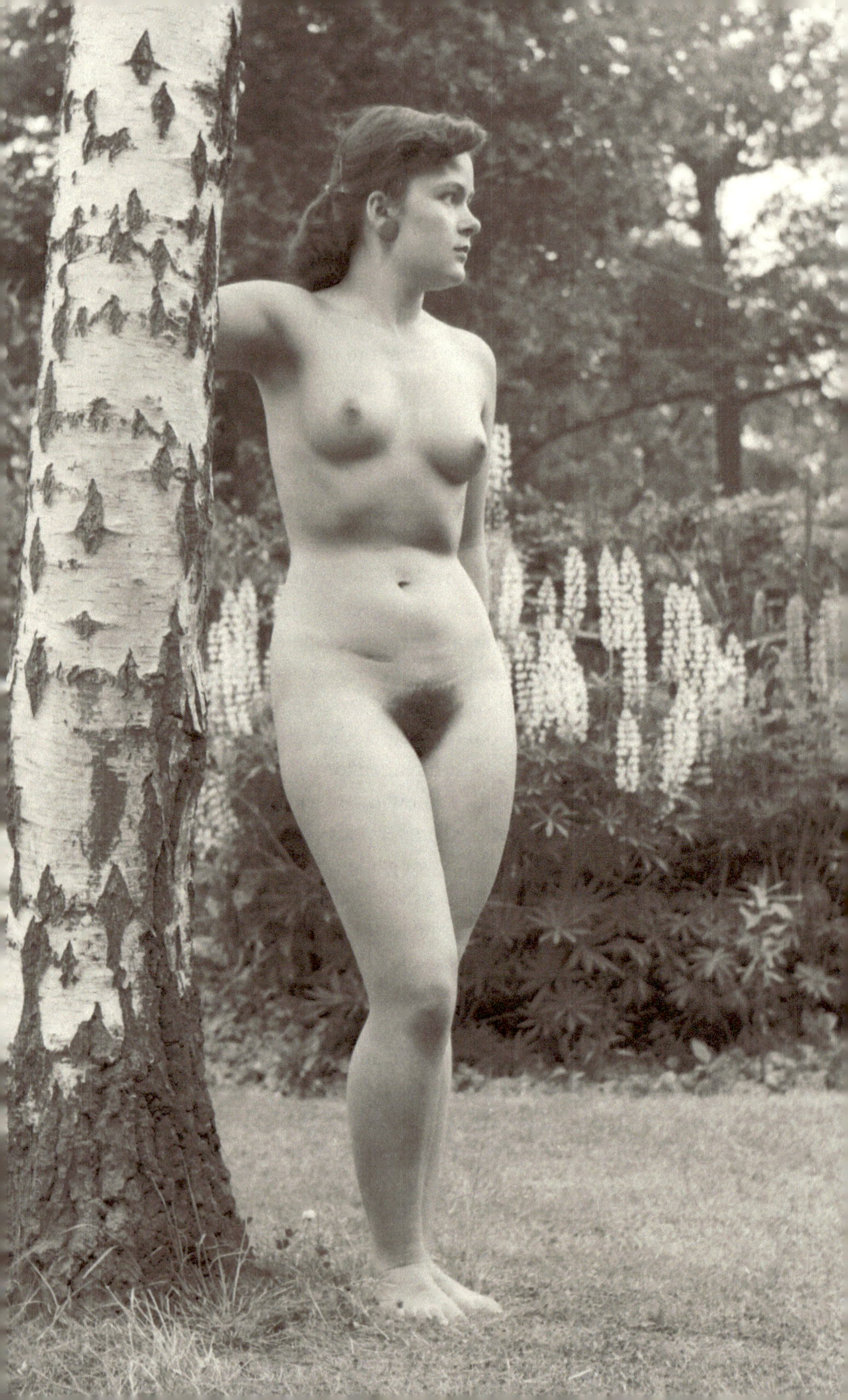

uncommon in young folk) to "show-off." I must admit that when I first became a practising Nudist I could not see the force of Indoor Nudism. It seemed to me the complete inversion of all that Nudism stood for. The general conditions of the usual Nudist camp appealed to me as being perfectly natural, but to be without clothes indoors quite pointless. I suppose that is the impression most people would get until experience and thought enlightened them. Actually an "air-bath" is the next best thing to a sun-bath (it is said that Benjamin Franklin used to spend an hour or so every morning in the nude), just as exposure to an ultra-violet or infra-red lamp is better than nothing when the sun is not available. Indoor games, such as Badminton or table tennis, and physical exercises can be enjoyed to greater advantage without clothes, too. But, above all, that sense of freedom, to which I have referred previously, makes it worthwhile on occasions. The same psychological atmosphere obtains in an indoor Nudist club as in the woods, and goes to prove that there is more in Nudism than just exposure of the skin to the sun.

It has taken some years for Nudism to be regarded as rational by even a proportion of our population. First it had to live down the stigma of an unbridled licence for immoral, or amoral, debauchees. As it became better understood it was freed from this libel and transferred from the plane of abhorrence to that of ridicule. Nudists were cranks and fanatics; a bit soft in the head or with "bees in the bonnet." Now we have reached the stage where the average person is liable to consider it "all right for those that like it." To be without

---

Left: *The Elusive Dryad.*

clothes indoors, however, is to lack the excuse of "sun-bathing," which has become a popular pastime, and requires a good deal more of explanation. Indeed, it is difficult to explain it simply and in a way which everyone can grasp. That is because so much has been made of the physical benefits and so little said about its psychological advantages. But I think this aspect is becoming better understood by degrees, and its general understanding will add tremendously to the case for Nudism as a whole.

On my title page I have quoted Sir Horace Walpole's saying: "When I cast off my clothes, I cast off my cares!" and this is really the keynote of this chapter. Conscious and subconscious handicaps can be shed with our clothes. Our minds can be freed at the same time as our bodies and a better balance gained all round. Nudism means freedom for body and soul, and no one can be really healthy and happy unless the two are in unison.

CHAPTER VI

Natural Selection

DAVID LLOYD GEORGE may live in History as "The Man who Won the Great War," but among his contemporaries he will probably be remembered for his aptitude in coining catchy phrases, and amongst the most pertinent was that "You cannot have an A.1 nation with a C.3 population." Since that obvious truism was given to the world, very little has been done to raise our own population to the A.1 class; but recently, with slum clearance, study of nutrition and improvements in child welfare, we have become more aware of the potentialities and needs of our national physique, and now we are about to have a "Fitter Britain" campaign under Government auspices. As with National Insurance and other sociological improvements Germany has set us an example, and she has some fifteen years' start of us, but it is all to the good that we have awakened to the situation. Germany became "body-conscious" soon after the end of the War, and we can see to-day the practical results of their hiking, camping, organised exercises and — Nudism. "Nacte-cultur" or "Nude-culture" was started in Germany with a view to the improvement of national physique, and the number of adherents in 1930 was estimated by a Berlin newspaper at 3,000,000 (three millions). Analysis of the results of examination of young men called up for military service in 1935 showed that 77 per cent. were passed as fit in 1935 as against

63.6 in 1913, a gain of 134 per cent. It may be quite fairly assumed, I think, that the physical improvement of the opposite sex was in proportion indeed, evidence of this was given when nine out of twelve events in the Women's World Games, held in London in 1934, were won by German girls.

Is it not likely that the spread of Nudism may have a similar effect on all those nations where it becomes popular? May we not hope that future generations of the British people will attain a standard of physical perfection many degrees higher than that general to-day? I think so. Human evolution has been progressing for thousands of years sometimes progress has paused or been diverted from its proper course, but the principal incentive has always been the desire to achieve the ideal, and upon the character of that ideal the trend of progress depends. The vague idea that we are all descended from monkeys, erroneously attributed to Darwin by the ignorant, doubtless originated from his great work, "The Origin of Species." Darwin, with great experience as a naturalist, traced the divergence of types and their subsequently stabilised characteristics by means of "natural selection" — that is to say, in order to survive, any creature had to become more and more adaptable to the conditions of its existence. Where the need for fleetness arose, either as a means of capturing prey or escaping from pursuers, the fleetest survived, the less fleet, presumably, either dying of starvation or being caught and destroyed by the pursuers. Hence arose the theory of "the survival of the fittest."

Arising out of this, or linked with it, was another theory, the influence of "Sexual Selection." To ensure progeny it is necessary not only to survive, but to secure a mate. Where the female of the species is so insignificant as to have no say in the matter, the stouter fighter would be able to take his pick, providing he could vanquish the rival males, but where a certain degree of selection is permitted to the females, mere bellicosity would be of little avail.

And so we see, in the case of birds, for instance, that beauty of plumage, ability to sing or in some way to attract the affections of the female, makes for the survival of a certain type.

Up to a point, Darwin proved both these theories, and it is only in domestic environment, where man decides on the ideal and selects the mates, that Natural Selection and Sexual Selection are thwarted. Man wants cows to give more milk and bullocks to produce more meat, sheep to give more wool and horses to run faster; and so, by the selection of mates, he produces the desired type instead of Nature or members of the actual species making the selection. So far as domesticated animals or plants are concerned, this may work out excellently, but when it comes to human beings it is rather a different matter. In the days of slavery, there was very little discrimination on the part of the slave-owner regarding the reproductive proclivities of his slaves; but in out-standing cases the same procedure was followed as by a breeder of animals. There were even plantations known as "slave farms," where, in addition to doing plantation work, the slaves were regarded as the producers of more slaves, and their physical attributes were considered in much the same way as among breeders of horses and cattle by the more enlightened (?) slave-owners.

In a free and democratic community the selection of mates is left to individuals, and we come back to Natural Selection and Sexual Selection. What influences the individual's choice of a mate? Propinquity is probably the greatest influence. Young men and women who are thrown together by circumstances and subject to the urge of sex are quite naturally likely to become mates either officially by marriage or even unofficially by cohabitation. Either party may be attracted by a handsome face, financial position, similarity of interests or dress. A girl or young man may spend all her, or his, available income on appearance, and the aid of the dressmaker or tailor may be enlisted in the securing of a mate. From the purely physical point of view, both parties will probably be in complete, or almost complete, ignorance of the partner's qualifications. What is more, the practical nature of those qualifications will scarcely be even considered. It is unfortunate that such qualifications, or the lack of them, can only be discovered after the intimacy of marriage.

This problem has been dealt with by writers on ideal states since the time of Sir Thomas More, who wrote, in 1556, in his "Utopia": "In choosing their wives they use a method that would appear to us very absurd and ridiculous, but it is constantly observed among them and is accounted perfectly consistent with wisdom. Before marriage, some grave matron presents the bride, naked, whether she is virgin or widow, to the bridegroom, and after that, some grave man presents the bride-groom, naked, to the bride. We, indeed, both laugh at this and condemn it as very indecent. But they, on the other hand, wondered at the folly of men of other nations, who, if they are to buy a horse of small value, are so cautious that they will see every part of him and take off both saddle and bridle and all his other tackle, that there may be no secret hid under any of them; and that yet, in the choice of a wife, on which depends the happiness or unhappiness of the rest of his life, a man should venture upon trust." Which, at least, is a logical way of looking at it, and comes from a man of great experience and understanding.

Bacon, however, did not agree with this, and in his "New Atlantis" (1626) he wrote: "I have read in a book of one of your men of a feigned commonwealth, where the married couple are permitted, before they contract, to see one another naked. This they dislike, for they think it a scorn to give a refusal after so familiar knowledge; but because of many hidden defects in men's and women's bodies, they have a more civil way; for they have near every town a couple of pools (which they call Adam and Eve's pools) where it is permitted to one of the friends of the man and another of the friends of the woman, to see them severally, both naked." This seems to me a far less satisfactory solution, as the matter is left to the judgment of friends, and if there is any delicacy to be considered, surely it is more natural for the parties interested to reveal their intimacies to each other, rather than to out-siders. Surely one who was very particular in this respect would feel somewhat embarrassed in the knowledge that his friend was familiar with his wife's nakedness, and vice versa in the case of a lady. What is really more important, however, is this: that the ideal which is to influence the trend of progress, as already referred to, should be one of physical perfection. Then sexual selection will automatically and inevitably bring about a general raising of the standard. I can conceive of no more likely way of ensuring this than the widespread practice of Nudism.

In previous chapters I have pointed out the opportunity and encouragement offered by Nudist camps or clubs for physical culture and the desire engendered for improved physical fitness. This applies particularly to the younger members. Vanity, which in some circumstances may be regarded as a vice, can, when modified by these conditions, become a virtue as it forms an incentive towards a higher ideal. Where the individual is deprived of the assistance of clothing to present a good appearance, he, or she, must fall back upon improving the body itself — and will certainly take steps to that end. Here we get a means of individual improvement; but the influence goes farther than this. Children and young people who develop in a Nudist "atmosphere" will adjust their sense of values accordingly. They will regard a beautiful body as of far greater value than beautiful clothes; strength and suppleness as finer accomplishments than witty conversation or the ability to absorb large quantities of alcohol. They will become accustomed to the respect and admiration of all members for those who have well-formed bodies and are capable of athletic feats. It must follow, when the time comes for them to select mates, physical perfection, with which they are thoroughly familiar, will influence their choice very considerably. I do not suggest that the ideal will revert to the "caveman" period. Mere "huskiness" and brute strength will not attract or invite envy. I think, rather, that the ideal will be more like that of the Ancient Greeks, which still remains the standard by which physical beauty may be judged. And it must be remembered that the Greeks did not worship the body alone. The coordination of body and mind, developed by many athletic sports, was regarded as essential. Many physical achievements depend largely upon a spiritual backing. Skill, endurance, the sense of fair-play, which we regard as the essence of sportsmanship, are the result of psychological training which may be observed in all great athletic events such as the Oxford and Cambridge boat race or a first-class amateur boxing bout. Courage, both physical and moral, will be developed amongst Nudists of both sexes and will form an integral part of the new ideal. Can there be any doubt that these conditions will have considerable effect upon the coming generation? Already one can see — I have seen — a changed attitude in those who have practised Nudism for a comparatively short period.

The proportion of practising Nudists in this country is a small one as yet, although it is growing rapidly, and the movement has not been in existence long enough to show very vital results; but if straws show the direction of the wind, there is sufficient evidence available to justify "great expectations." First a general physical improvement in individuals of all ages and both sexes; then the acceptance of new ideals and, subsequently, a fresh generation from "naturally selected" parents superior in form and fitness to those who have gone before. At present I know of only four "Nudist babies," but they are all excellent examples. They may, later on, have the usual childish complaints, which one is inclined to take for granted, like distemper in puppies, but they certainly promise to make fine specimens as they grow up.

With the change of ideals may be found a solution of the publicly-deplored fall in the birth-rate, although, personally, I regard this more as a matter of economics than a moral or physical problem. In cases of genuine sterility a more healthy and vigorous life might contribute to some amelioration of these conditions, but where methods of birth control are exercised deliberately, the motive is usually an economic one. The

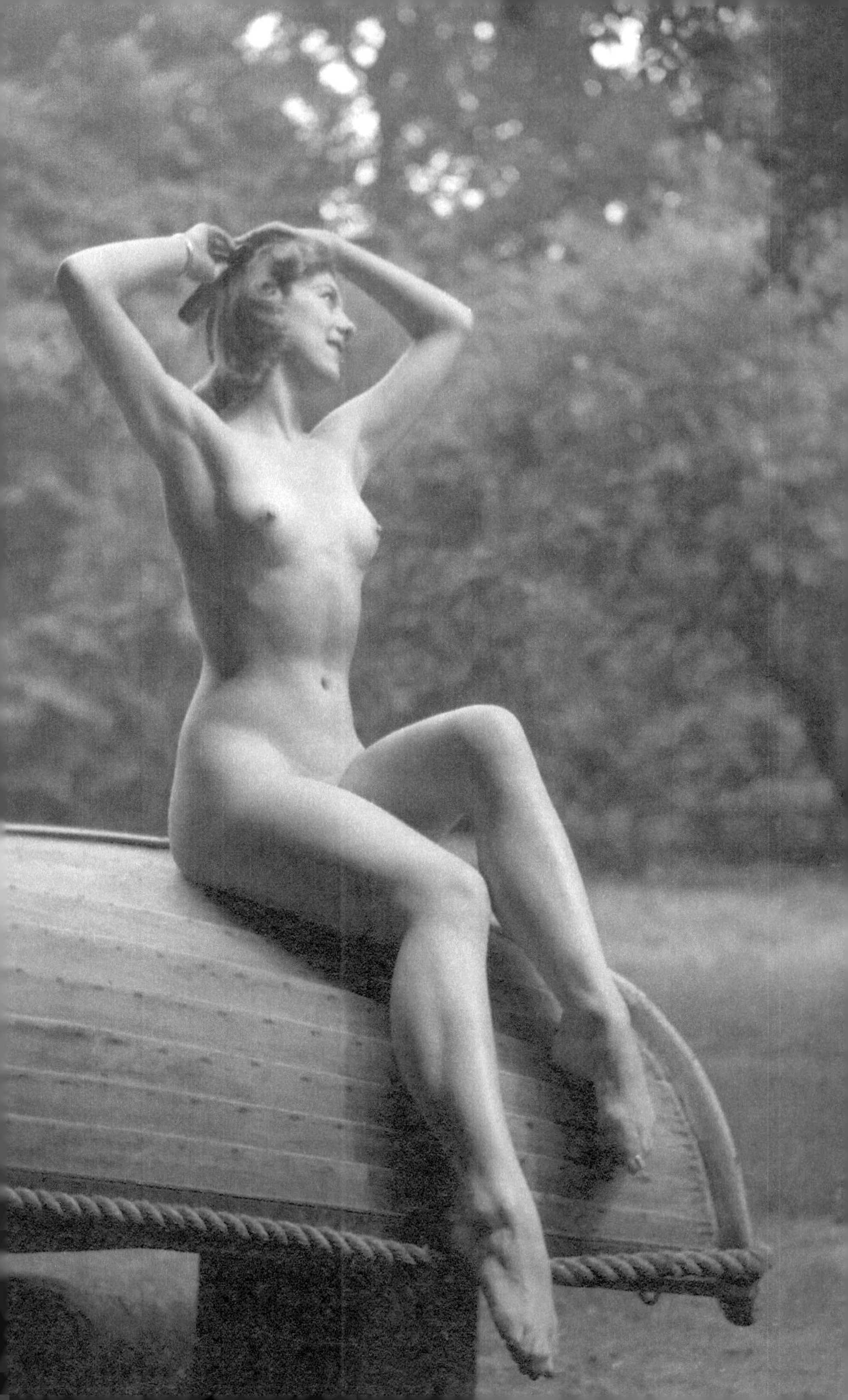

Eugenists' desire for "fewer and better births," however, may well be met by the natural selection of "fewer and better" parents. I can say, with personal knowledge, that the question of babies is not ignored by Nudists. Although they are not all parents, I have noticed a more than usual interest in babies shown by Nudists, and nearly all the Nudists I know are child-lovers. Naturally, a little extra fuss is made of a new baby in a Nudist community, and the sight of a few months' old infant rolling on a blanket in the sun (sans swaddling) is rather stirring. I am not going to say that Nudism will have any marked effect on the raising of the birth-rate, but it does suggest an improvement in quality, if not quantity, and this is one good reason for enthusiastic Eugenists supporting the movement.

The future lies in the hands of the younger generation. The older folk can hardly expect to re-make their bodies, even though they may effect some improvement; but the youth of both sexes can mould themselves on ideal lines, and they will be the parents of the next generation. Nudism may be regarded as contributing to a finer nation physically, both practically and ideally, and the fact that it induces admiration for beautiful bodies must, in itself, affect the selection of marital partners in the potential parents of tomorrow. There are people who object to photographs of the male and female form in the nude. I see no sound reason why a beautiful photograph should be regarded as any more indecent or pornographic than a beautiful statue or picture. So far as training the mind to regard the body with more respect and to induce ambition in this respect, there seems every reason to regard actual reproductions from

Left: *Pose and Poise.*

life as good propaganda. They may be viewed as examples of how beautiful the body can be, and should be, and the first thing required by would-be idealists is some concrete idea of the ideal they have to aim at.

I believe it is accepted in some circles that a woman expecting a baby should be surrounded by beautiful pictures, ornaments and articles of furniture — somewhat on the principle of Jacob setting up the speckled rods at the watering troughs that the cattle might bring forth "ring straked, speckled and spotted," and so add to his share of Laban's flocks. In my opinion the observation of beautiful bodies in the nude, or really good photographs of them, offer the greatest incentive to physical improvement. If by such means we can raise ideals and induce greater respect for physical beauty, it may be regarded as a worthy achievement.

It has been said that "beauty lies in the eyes of the beholder" and any indecency or wickedness to be found in the nude body undoubtedly lies in the mind of the beholder. The familiarity with the human form which is common to all practising Nudists disposes of any erotic excitement or curiosity, but it in no way diminishes appreciation of its beauty, and, since all sorts of figures may be seen in a Nudist camp, it is a definite aid to discrimination.

On more than one occasion I have written about the pleasing effect of a well-tanned skin; I have said that a golden-brown body does not seem "naked" in the same way that the dead-white skin of an unexposed body may do. To be perfectly honest, which always has been my aim in all my writings, I must admit that this opinion must now be amended. One of the clubs of which I am a member gave a tea party in the woods last summer, and amongst the visitors who were entertained were a young married couple. The man was well-shaped and tawny, but his wife was of the palest ivory hue. Her figure was the most beautiful it has been my good fortune to see since I have been connected with the movement. She looked like an exquisite Tanagra figurine, and was as graceful in her movements as she was beautiful in body. She had long hair, and, before I had heard her speak, I told my wife that I was sure from her face that she had a beautiful voice. I proved to be right in my deduction, and, although she did not talk much, it was a real joy to hear her speak. Here was an example upon which the next generation might well be modelled, and I think that every beholder felt just a little uplifted at the sight. With more and more examples of this type, surely the ambition of others must be raised and efforts made to improvement in the individual and a greater discrimination in the selection of a mate. A truly "natural selection" which must bring into the world a more beautiful generation if the logical sequence is allowed to follow.

With all that may be done officially to secure a "fitter Britain," I believe that Nudism will have more effect on Britain in the future than mere housing, feeding and exercising. At least I honestly hope so.

CHAPTER VII

Nudity in Fiction

MANY WRITERS HAVE dealt with nudity from various aspects and the list would be far too long to be included here. There is now quite an appreciable number of books on the Nudist Movement as considered in the preceding pages, but I want to refer to a few examples of how writers of fiction have viewed the subject.

There must have existed some prejudice against the complete exposure of a woman's body even in the time of Plato, because in his "Republic" he thought it necessary to argue against such prejudices as follows: — "And the man who laughs at naked women, whilst performing their exercises for the sake of what is best, reaps the empty fruit of a ridiculous wisdom and in no respect knows, as appears at what he laughs nor why he does it. For that ever was and will be deemed a noble saying that what is most advantageous for the public is handsome and what is more hurtful is ugly." He said a good deal more to the same point, but we need not go into that now.

The first purely fictional reference I can remember was a novel called "The Storm of London." It was written some thirty years ago, and described the effects of a storm which in some miraculous way destroyed every vestige of textile fabric which could be used for clothing. Immediately after the storm, the whole population found themselves naked as they were born; dukes and duchesses, ministers and milkmen — all were in a state of immutable nudity. At first there was a feeling of shock, as the nude duchess was waited upon by a nude footman and the duke's valet found it impossible to lay out his master's clothes for the day. In a very short time, however, everyone got used to it, and business and social events went on without a hitch.

In "Simon Called Peter," Robert Keable was not free from an appeal to the erotic instinct, but perhaps one of the most chaste passages in the book is the description of Julie's entrance from the bathroom wearing nothing but a rosebud: — "She was still half-wet from the water and her sole dress was a rosebud which she had just tucked into her hair. She stood there, laughing, a perfect vision of unblushing, natural loveliness." And later: — "It was exactly Julie, who sat there unashamed in her nakedness, Peter thought. She had kept the soul of a child through everything, and it could burst through the outer covering of the woman who had tasted of the tree of knowledge of good and evil, and laugh in the sun." Julie naked was far more natural and innocent than Julie clothed.

Warner Fabian in "Flaming Youth" gives a picture of modern American youth, more or less equivalent to our "Bright Young Things" or fast set. One night, after a lightning-stroke, all the lights go out during a big house-party and someone suggests bathing in the pool in semi-darkness without costumes. The idea seems to be regarded as daring and sufficiently wicked to impart a "kick" to the proceedings, but before they all have time to enter the pool there is a shriek, the restored lights are switched on, and it is discovered that one girl has been hauled from the water unconscious and half-drowned. All the "kick" comes from the superfluity of alcohol already imbibed, and the participants are all much cooler and more restrained after the event than before.

Pride of body is shown in Oliver Onions' "Story of Louie." Louie, the daughter of an aristocratic lady who married (on account of his magnificent physique) a prize-fighter who has posed as a model for her sculpture, becomes a professional model. One evening, while she is posing, a friend of the artist unexpectedly enters the studio and she recognises him as the man who, some years before, had inspired her with passionate love — unknown to himself, be it said. She glows in an ecstasy of pride and joy that he should view the beauty of her body in its entirety. Her heart sings that this is the greatest thing that could have happened to her; that however little thought he may have had of her before, he must now realise and remember her as a vision of physical perfection. Just another point of view, and it should be remembered that she is a well-educated girl of good breeding.

To the hero and heroine of Richard Aldington's "All Men are Enemies" it comes quite naturally to take a bathe in a little cove in the Mediterranean, even though they have no costumes, and they plunge in together, swim, and afterwards bask in the sun without the slightest embarrassment. To them it seems "only natural."

Although "Sunwards," by George C. Foster, is really an account of a family whose fortunes are linked with transportation — first railways, then motor-cars, and finally with aeroplanes — it is described on the jacket as a "Novel about Nudism." Personally, I found this comment a little misleading, but it does show very simply and sincerely how a daughter starts by discarding her clothes to swim and sun-bathe, and later to form a camping-party of girl and boy friends who find a healthy joy in freeing themselves of clothes and a camaraderie typical of a Nudist camp. It is a book which shows sympathy with, and understanding of, the Nudist movement. I believe Mr. Foster is himself a genuine Nudist and has written articles on his actual experiences.

Nudity is shown in excellent perspective and with considerable eloquence by Clarence Buddington Kelland in "Jahala." This is the story of a girl born and bred on an American farm, with the soul of a dancer. She is one of those gifts of Nature, an inspired artist. Whether her parentage and environment would conduce to such a prodigy it is not for us to say, but listen to her first experience of the freedom of nudity: "Something moved her, urged her. She knew a surge of happiness, of instinctive joy of life. She got to her feet and poised, unconsciously, without even baby affectation... And then she danced. A pixy she swayed to and fro, arms aloft, head back, feet lifting to some cadence heard by her ears alone... She did not know why, never could explain why even under her father's terrible inquisition, but she sat down with childish deliberation and removed her left shoe, and then her right shoe. Her stockings followed, so that her bare toes knew the delightful softness and coolness of the grass. Her little dress, her over-abundant underclothing, fell beside them, and she stood there beside that silvery water, fresh from mountain springs, an infant nymph bursting with incomprehensible joy... And then she danced, danced the dance of the worship of the Sun god, to the god residing in the trees, to the goddess of the stream... It was spontaneous as the gushing of water from a spring is spontaneous, as the song from the throat of a bird — and as beautiful, as innocent, as bewitching." Her dancing is brought to an abrupt end by the heavy hand of her father, who, after administering an almost brutal beating, makes her swear upon the Bible that never again will she do such a wicked, shameful, degrading thing. The contrast between the natural innocence and beauty of the child's spirit and the narrow-mindedness of the bigoted father is very striking. It is a just commentary on the average attitude of those who have no breadth of understanding and whose intelligence is limited to their own environment and training.

In earlier pages I have referred to the difference, from an erotic point of view, between nudity and semi-nudity. This is exemplified in "Grand Hotel," that famous, best-selling novel which most of us have read or seen adapted on the stage or the screen. Here, Flammchen, the young, "flapperish" secretary-typist, is gay and irresponsible. She likes to have a "good time" and is occasionally prepared to make herself agreeable to gentlemen with well-filled pocket-books and to take life as it comes. She is so live and real that one feels that Vicky Baum must have drawn her direct from life; or perhaps she is a composite character built from observation of several models. She has no feeling of shame for nudity; indeed, she is justifiably proud of her body; but when Herr Preysing, with whom she has agreed to travel to England on certain terms, wishes to make love to her in the hotel bedroom, she has her limits. Her clothing has been removed and lies neatly folded upon a chair, "As tidily as a school-girl," says Vicky Baum; nothing is left but her shoes and stockings. "Leave your stockings on, though. It looks so pretty," said Preysing. "No," said Flammchen, "I should feel horrid. I can't be in nothing but shoes and stockings!" Here again, one sees the chastity of complete nudity which, in itself, has nothing of the lewd or erotic compared with semi-nudity.

Few, if any, good fiction writers have fallen into the fallacy that the naked body of a woman represents lust and lewdness. To give allurement the body must be partly clothed, or at least decorated, and a certain amount of appeal made to imagination and curiosity. Writers of novels which may be considered in the erotic class — and there are plenty of them — usually describe with gusto the intimate details of their heroines' underwear. In some cases the lover is invited to assist in the disrobing, or partial disrobing, of his inamorata, and he appears to get a tremendous thrill from the observation of "two ivory orbs nestling in a wealth of foamy lace," or catches his breath as "a soft rounded shoulder" emerges from its covering. "Soft lights and sweet music," the shimmer of silk or the revealing concealment of lace and frills, are all aids to the erotic atmosphere.

Writers of an earlier age did not beat about the bush when describing the charms of their alluring ladies. Fielding, Sterne, and — particularly — playwrights of the Restoration period, had no false modesty and discussed the physical features of their females with a candour almost brutal. But they never regarded the nudity of a woman as a stimulus to love-making.

Writers, probably, show less interest in the nude than sculptors and painters — which is perhaps only natural — while the latter regard the female form with the same consideration as they might a tree, or a cloud, or any other component part of a picture — from its aesthetic merits alone. This is not to say that writers, painters and sculptors are anchorites and

misogynists. On the contrary, their sensitivity, imagination
and responsiveness are usually more lively than those of the
average layman. The true artist, however, has always a sense of
perspective and proportion, and an understanding of human
impulses. Love scenes in fiction vary from the sickly sweet
to the violently passionate, from the fantastically romantic
to the sordidly real; but never, to my knowledge, has nudity
been featured as an erotic stimulant either to the reader or
the character.

Although, as I have said, there are already a number of
books (mostly American) on Nudism as distinct from Nudity,
there seems to be very little fiction dealing with the subject.
Perhaps the time is not yet ripe. Neither the general public
nor the majority of writers are familiar with the realities of the
movement, and there is, of course, the danger of the atmosphere becoming propagandist, which is fatal to all forms of art.
I have read extracts from one book of this kind which seemed to
me merely silly. It was not good literature, and it was not good
propaganda either. On the other hand, there is one novel which
introduces a phase of genuine Nudism and which impressed
me very favourably. It is written by a clever and experienced
author, James Laver, and includes an account of a German
"Gelande" or Nudist centre. The book is in a humorously
satirical vein, interwoven with shrewd observation and insight,
and although the description of "Himmelheim" is amusing, it
is substantially true to reality, and those who have visited Herr
Zimmermann's establishment at Klingberg, or have studied
Frances and Mason Merrill's "Among the Nudists" and other
first-hand accounts of this famous German centre, will have
little doubt that "Himmelheim" is drawn from Klingberg and

"Professor Kirschwasser" from Herr Zimmermann. Assuming that this is so, and allowing for a certain amount of poetic licence, it is something much more than a mere burlesque. It may be regarded as a serious and sensible portrayal of the aims and atmosphere of a typical Nudist community.

"Nymph Errant" has had such a wide circulation, in addition to being presented in dramatic form in a West-End theatre, that it is more than likely that many of my readers will be familiar with it; but for the benefit of those who are not, and in order that those who have read it, but know nothing of practical Nudism, may appreciate the application, I want to review some of the essential points. Evangeline (the heroine) has left school in Switzerland, but on her way home to Oxford she meets various young men with whom she has a series of amorous adventures. At a studio party in Paris, where there is an excess of cocktail-drinking, and dancing and petting take place amongst a company of girls and young men in various states of undress (two girls dance together, "one in a diaphanous chemise, and the other in a *pantaloon* of black lace, her adolescent torso marble-white under the harsh glare of the lights"), a young German tells Evangeline that he has a distaste for Paris because it makes him feel "sodden with sex." "Clothes," says he, "are designed solely to outline the figure, to tempt the eye, to set the imagination working. We should all be much better without any clothes at all." Evangeline suggests that his ideal must be almost realised here since none of the party is wearing many clothes, but the young German disagrees. "They are wearing too few or too many. Complete nudity is chaste, but a transparent *dentelle* is the very opposite to nudity." He tells her of Himmelheim and she agrees to

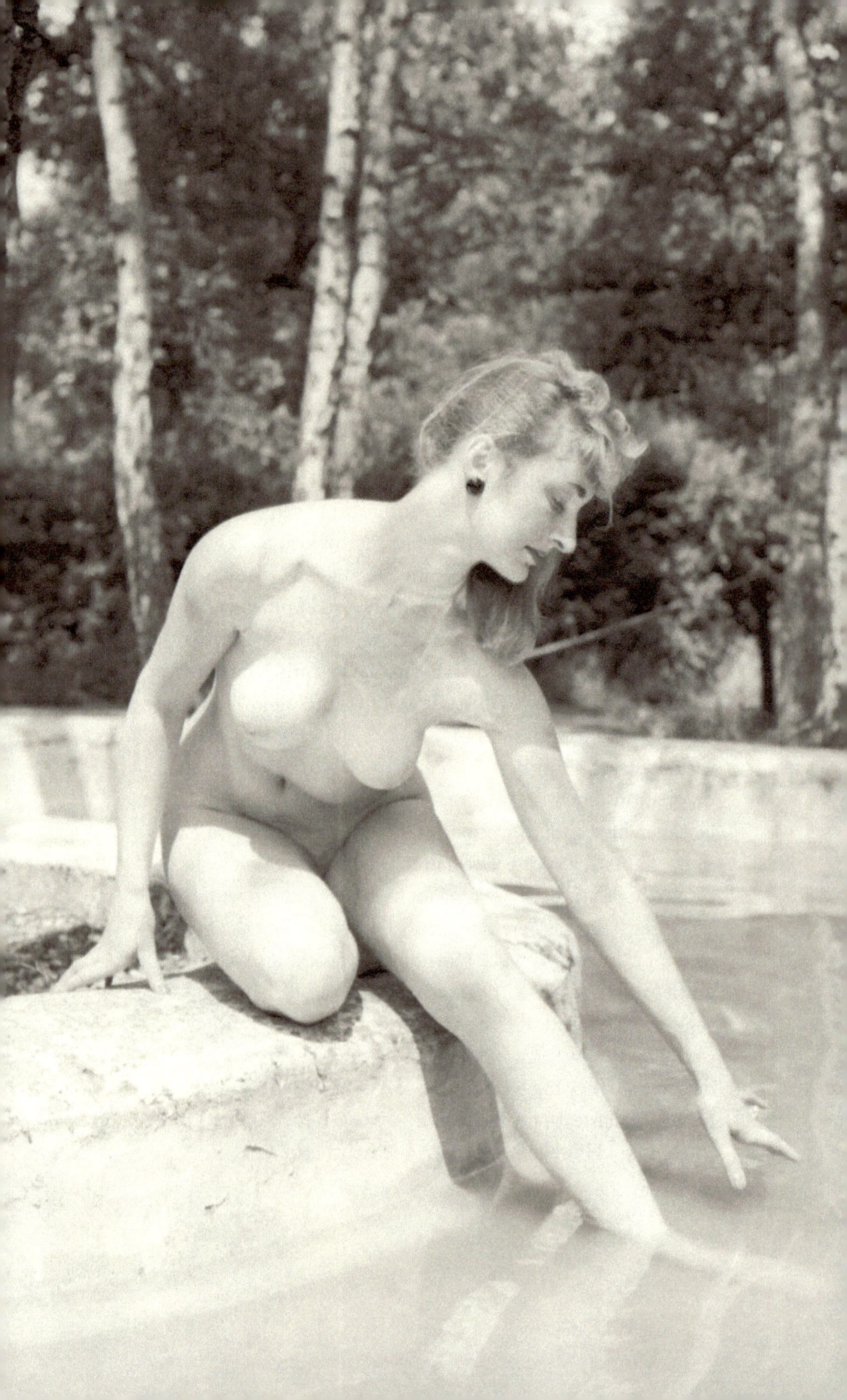

accompany him there — not as his mistress, but as a comrade seeking a cleaner, healthier, saner life. Although, thanks to her adventures, she is no longer an unsophisticated school-girl, she receives rather a shock when, on arrival at Himmelheim, she finds a girl of about eighteen setting the table in the dining-hall — completely nude. She is introduced to this girl, who shakes hands with her and greets her in a quite conventional manner without the slightest trace of embarrassment, and offers to show her to her room so that she can remove her clothes and be comfortable. After undressing, with a certain amount of reluctance, she returns to the dining-room, where she is amazed to meet one of her school-friends. Bertha, it seems, has come to Himmelheim as companion to an aunt who is an enthusiastic Nudist. The idea was repugnant to Bertha at first, but now she, too, has become an enthusiast.

Actually this phase of Evangeline's adventures is the most striking of them all. It is so entirely "different." She learns quickly. After elaborate dinners at Deauville and in Paris, the plain food; simple dishes, strictly vegetarian, and absence of any form of alcohol; seems a bit dull, but she soon finds an atmosphere of healthy gaiety. "So the days passed, so quickly that Evangeline lost count of them, aware only of a growing physical well-being, the placid contentment of a healthy open-air life." And later: — "Her skin grew tougher and more elastic, and gradually changed its colour; the white phantom became a brown gazelle. The flesh grew firmer, the joints more supple, the separate parts of her body took on a life of their

Left: *Calm Waters.*

own." The description of how Evangeline finds herself during this return to Nature is very sound.

The impish, fun-poking characteristic of most of the book here gives way to sincere and convincing expression of the changes effected by this new life. I do not think Mr. Laver, with all his cleverness, could have written these passages unless he had had actual personal experience and had felt the same mutability as that which he attributes to his heroine. Even when he returns to his epigrammatic dialogue, the effect of his experience is evident. Vladimir, the Russian Nihilist, who eschews all forms of discipline and organisation, lets fall some very significant remarks. "… here no woman can be better than her neighbour, except by the accident of a beautiful body or as the reward of strenuous training." How true a comment on the fundamentals of the Nudist Movement! It is not until a whimsical fancy induces Evangeline to make herself an abbreviated skirt from the leaves of a wild vine that the old erotic atmosphere returns and eventually leads to a liaison similar to those she had previously experienced. When Heinz, the young German, sees her: "The self-consciousness which it was Professor Kirshwasser's proudest boast to have banished from Himmelheim returned with such force that he would gladly have imitated his companion's example and made himself an apron of leaves." The inevitable ensues. But not at the Gelande. They arrange to leave Himmelheim and meet at a country house in the neighbourhood. Here we may leave them; they no longer illustrate the theme of this book. "Behind was Sparta, before was Sybaris."

I think the few examples I have chosen throw an interesting sidelight on the subject by illustrating the views of fiction writers, which, on the whole, link up quite logically with those of writers from the scientific point of view. The lack of erotic stimulus, as compared with clothing or partial clothing; the spiritual effects of nudity and the general ignorance or mis-understanding suffered by those who have had no experience or have given insufficient thought to the subject, are exem-plified. Just as novels have thrown light on various political or socio-logical problems, or at least proved provocative of thought, so the writers quoted may help us to understand better the question of nudity and its reactions. Incidentally, they will be found to give disinterested support to the views and convictions which I have expressed in earlier pages.

CHAPTER VIII

The Philosophy of Nudism

WEBSTER'S DICTIONARY DEFINES Philosophy as "The love of wisdom as leading to the search for it"; or, alternatively, "The general principles, laws or causes that furnish the rational explanation of any thing." Possessing "a love of wisdom as leading to the search for it," I have studied Nudism from all angles, and in the foregoing chapters I have endeavoured to "furnish the rational explanation." My main object has been to clear away some of the fallacies and misunderstandings which even now exist in the minds of many people who have had no opportunity of studying the realities of the subject.

I do not expect every reader of this book immediately to become an ardent Nudist. If I have succeeded in arousing interest in the merits of the movement and establishing a realisation of the *bona fides* of genuine Nudists, I shall feel that I have done some really useful work. I believe that those who have read Chapters I to VII will have come to the conclusion that, so far from being cranks and faddists, Nudists are really very sane people with definite, logical reasons for acting as they do.

What does the practice actually amount to when properly investigated and analysed? The living, for at least part of the

time, of a simple, healthy, happy, *natural* life! There you have
the philosophy of Nudism in a nutshell. Nothing wildly revolutionary, like Communism or Fascism; nothing depraved
or immoral; nothing that can in any way be harmful to others
or regarded logically as unnatural. I have shown, in Chapter
IV, how Nature needs certain conditions to carry out her
work efficiently, and how the periodical exposure of the body
to sun and air helps to provide these conditions. The very
sceptical may disagree with my conclusions; may consider
that it is quite unnecessary to take regular air-baths. Well, it
is not so very many years ago that a man or woman taking an
ordinary bath ("wetting themselves all over") was regarded as
mentally abnormal and the practice as eccentric and dangerous
to health. Even to-day, personal hygiene is so imperfectly
understood in some circles that excessive washing is regarded
either as affectation or as evidence of weak-mindedness. Here is
an instance of ignorance which I came across quite recently. A
labourer, quite a decent man, was telling me that occasionally
his daughter and two sons borrowed the mother's washing
tub to bathe themselves "all over." His comment was: "I don't
mind. I don't believe it doos 'em no 'arm; doos 'em good, I
reckon!" Not that he, presumably, would be prepared to go
to such extreme lengths!

Within my own memory the possession of a bathroom was
confined to the well-to-do, and regarded rather as the possession of a motor-car was a few years ago — as an indication of
social status. The Englishman is regarded as almost fanatical
with regard to his desire for soap and water and ventilation;
but this is a relatively modern phase of English character, and
a great deal of prejudice had to be overcome before it was

accepted as being the correct thing. There seems very little doubt, from the assurances of travellers and reliable observers, that the cleanest nation in the world is the Japanese. Long before bodily cleanliness was appreciated in Europe, "all-over" bathing was an established practice in Japan, and was carried out with extreme care and thoroughness. Incidentally, there was no pseudo-shame in exposing the body to the view of members of the opposite sex. Families, and even strangers, bathed together in the nude without the slightest embarrassment. The same attitude applies to Scandinavia and Finland. I have mentioned in another place Du Chaillu's description of the village bath-house in Norway, where the whole community congregated for steam-baths, and sometimes rolled in the snow afterwards. Yet the chastity and good sense of these nations is unimpeachable.

The fact — referred to in Chapter II — that in Australia nude "sun-baking" has been publicly approved and that the municipal authorities of at least one of our own seaside resorts permit the nudity of children on the public sands, suggests that a better understanding by governing bodies is at hand. Since I began this book, I have learnt from the National daily Press that in the new school to be built by the London County Council at Peckham, "boys and girls will have separate paddling pools with showers. The children will undress before they enter. Leading off from the pools will be screened courts, where the children will be permitted to run naked for several minutes after their paddle every day." The aims of these progressive and enlightened authorities are, basically, the aims of all Nudists — the achievement of health and fitness by natural means. Nudists rejoice in the awakened interest of the Government in the campaign for "a fitter Britain" the splendid efforts of the late Mrs. Bagot Stack, resulting in the establishment of the "Women's League of Health and Beauty," and the wonderful way in which her daughter, Prunella, has carried on the good work. Miss Stack stated over the Radio recently that the organisation started with sixteen girls and now has a membership of 120,000! When sufficient time has elapsed for the benefits of these movements to be properly appreciated, the pioneers will, doubtless, be regarded with pride and gratitude by the Nation at large — if later corners have not, in the. meantime, usurped the honour due to them.

My suggestion in Chapter VI that a wider spread of Nudism would set up new ideals and lead to a greater appreciation of physical fitness and more ambitious efforts to attain it, is also confirmed by later reading in the Press. A writer in the *Daily Telegraph*, next to *The Times* the soundest and least sensational of any of our daily newspapers, said: "The formation of a favourable public opinion is perhaps the most important factor in the whole problem. If only a fashion for fitness and a pride in physique can be engendered in the British people, the battle is as good as won." Another tribute to the philosophy of Nudism. But "Man cannot live by bread alone," and while the physical aspect of Nudism is of the greatest importance, there is more in the philosophy of Nudism than the ideal of physical beauty and physical strength. The emancipation of the mind and its natural development is just as important as the emancipation and development of the body. The blowing-away of mental cobwebs and the suppling and strengthening of individual thought is manifestly aided by the freedom and ease of the Nudist atmosphere.

I have dealt with "The Tyranny of Fashion," and this is a phase of clothes-consciousness which shows how the mind can be fettered and smothered by the clothes complex no less than the body. Clothes have their uses; in our climate, particularly, they are definitely needed as protection from the elements. It would take many generations of one hundred per cent. Nudists to make us entirely independent of clothes; but we must not overlook the fact that, mainly, clothes are symbolic. Symbolic of modesty, although I have shown that this aspect is really absurd on analysis; symbolic of class distinction — it seems ironical that the breeding of man or woman should be gauged by badges of rank rather than upon individual behaviour; and symbolical of national attitude. The Nudist's desire is to take clothes for what they are worth, but to deny them artificial values which cannot be established by logical reasoning.

As I have pointed out, Nudists are not savages. They appreciate the real advantages of civilisation and modern progress, but they have a keen perception of proportion. They see no reason why a healthy, natural life should not be enjoyed *pari passu* with inventions and productions which may make life easier and More pleasant. Surely this is a reasonable attitude of mind? So far as health and fitness are concerned, practically all modern scientists, and many of the ancient ones, are ranged on their side.

Personal association will prove that, morally and intellectually, Nudists compare favourably with almost any other types or groups. And the true Nudist, however enthusiastic he may be, does not proselytise. If you are genuinely interested in the Movement, he will be pleased to discuss it with you; to give you sound information and to answer reasonable questions to

Readers of this book who are already Nudists will, I hope, realise that these comments are made with a sincere desire for continuing the success already gained. Readers who, hitherto, have been ignorant of what the movement really means will, I hope, see that there really is "a case for" Nudism when calmly and carefully considered. More than this, I neither ask nor hope for.

The End

WOLFBAIT
UNDER THE COUNTER CULTURE

ALSO AVAILABLE

Cinema au Naturel
A history of nudist film.

Miniten: Rules of the Game
Invented in the 1930s, Miniten is
a tennis-like game played by naturists.

Naked as Nature Intended
The epic tale of a nudist picture by Pamela Green, with
photographs by Douglas "Dambuster" Webb, DFM.

The Naked Truth About Harrison Marks
The notorious biography by Franklyn Wood.

Past Masters of the Nude
An illustrated bibliography of nude photography books
published in England from 1896 to 1960.

Slide Show
A luscious look at the photographic
slides of Harrison Marks.

X-ray Specs and Other Vintage Ads
A unique treasure chest of vintage advertising,
full of tease and prurient silliness.

Doing Rude Things
The history of the British sex film.

THE STEPHEN GLASS COLLECTION

Amazons of Yesteryear
A rare, action-packed collection of images of wrestling
women of the 1940s and 1950s.

Beauty Off-Duty
Relaxed, everyday moments caught on camera.

Naked in the Menagerie
A playful look at Eve accompanied by her animal friends.

Nudist Camp Follies — volumes 1 and 2
An intimate look at the natural
and free atmosphere in Sun Clubs.

Nymphs and Naiads
Beauty unadorned and outdoors.

Poise and Pose
A magnificent series of photographs
of female beauty taken in the studio.

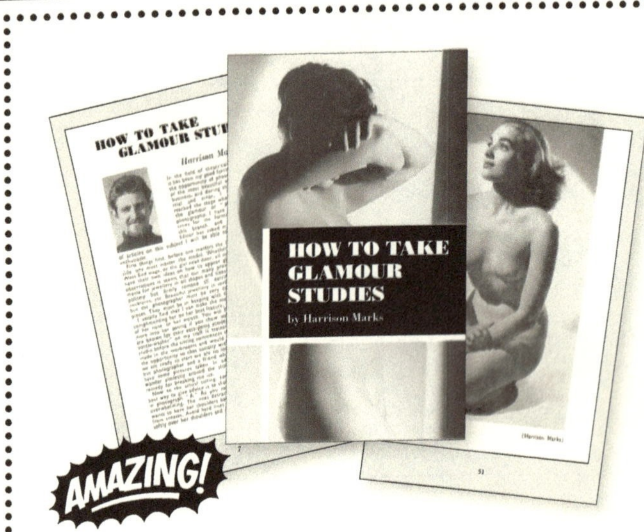

HOW TO TAKE
GLAMOUR
STUDIES
by Harrison Marks
AMAZING!